True Stories

Nonfiction Literacy in the Primary Classroom

Christine Duthie

Stenhouse Publishers
York, Maine

Stenhouse Publishers, 431 York Street, York, Maine 03909

Credits
Page 38–39: 1988. *The Unhuggables.* Vienna, VA: National Wildlife Federation. All rights reserved. Reprinted by permission.
Page 89–90: Gloria Houston. 1992. *My Great-Aunt Arizona.* New York: HarperCollins. Reprinted by permission.
Page 103–104: Don Brown. 1993. *Ruth Law Thrills a Nation.* New York: Ticknor and Fields. Reprinted by permission.
Page 133–135: Copyright © 1995 by Scholastic Inc. *Scholastic News.* New York: 51 (7), pp. 1 and 4.

Library of Congress Cataloging-in-Publication Data
Duthie, Christine
      True stories : nonfiction literacy in the primary classroom /
Christine Duthie.
            p.   cm.
      Includes bibliographical references (p.) and indexes.
      ISBN 1-57110-026-1 (alk. paper)
      1. Prose literature—Study and teaching (Primary) 2. Language
arts (Primary) 3. Children—Books and reading.   I. Title.
LB1527.D88 1996
372.6—dc20   96-34170
                            CIP

Cover and interior design by Martha Drury
Cover photograph by the author
Manufactured in the United States of America on acid-free paper
99 98 97 96 8 7 6 5 4 3 2

Contents

To my dad, who taught me to find pride and joy in hard work

Preface

Like many educators, for the past ten years I have been involved in the transformation that has taken place in language arts instruction in elementary classrooms. I have joined with other teachers in a grassroots movement to create holistic, child-centered classrooms. This involvement has given my teaching new direction—and raised new questions. It has also made me eager to go to school each day and confront the next challenge.

During this period, I did graduate work at the University of New Hampshire, where I encountered many of the leaders in the early reading and writing movement: Jane Hansen, Donald Murray, Donald Graves, Tom Romano, Linda Rief, Jack Wilde, Mark Milliken, Ellen Blackburn-Karelitz, Carol Avery, Susan Stires, Tom Newkirk, and Paula Flemming. At conferences I was fortunate to hear Nancie Atwell, Lucy Calkins, Ken Goodman, Yetta Goodman, Ralph Fletcher, Frank Smith, Georgia Heard, Bobbi Fisher, Patrick Shannon, Peter Johnston, Richard Allington, Susan Ohanian, Jerry Harste, David Elkind, and Mary Ellen Giacobbe. These pioneers have grounded my thoughts and shaped my philosophy.

Although I write as a first-grade teacher, I do not intend this book to be used as a manual for first grade. My research has developed over a five- to ten-year-period in a school with a heterogeneous population. I have rediscovered a familiar truth: children develop in different ways and along different developmental paths. Therefore, with each unique group of children, my teaching varies and their progress in nonfiction literacy varies. Some parts of this book will be appropriate with children from kindergarten to third grade.

I discuss a number of ways to incorporate nonfiction into reading and writing workshop mini-lessons and routines. Young nonfiction readers move beyond "encyclopedia text," and young writers beyond "the facts" to view nonfiction as a unique genre rich in possibilities. I pay special attention to the socially significant nonfiction writing called biography. My goal is to offer new perspectives and new ideas that open the doors of the delightful world of nonfiction to all young readers and writers.

Acknowledgments

I would not have found the world of writing without the work and love of many people. A poor speller with less than acceptable handwriting, I never wrote for pleasure as a child. My experience in elementary and secondary school convinced me, through painful demonstration, that if the mechanics weren't perfect, my writing wasn't worth reading. When as an adult I discovered computers and word processing, I found a magical playground I had never imagined could exist. But far more significant than technology are the people with whom I have worked and on whom I have relied. They believed in me and encouraged me to grow, and without them this book would not have been possible. My sincere and heartfelt thanks to all of them, but especially to Michelle Kolodij and Carole Grove for their tolerance, humor, and help in the library; Ellie Zimet for her work in the early stages of the research; my fellow graduate students at the University of New Hampshire Writing Project for their ongoing friendship and inspiration; the University of New Hampshire Graduate Writing Program for helping me learn about real learning and express my own; *Language Arts* and *The Reading Teacher* for providing a forum for teachers' writing; Don and Minnie May Murray for an unforgettable summer of backporch conversation; Jane Hansen for her work, inspiration, and common sense, and for always making time; Carolyn Lange, my principal, for wisdom, support, gentle advice, and pedagogical freedom; Gayla Miller, coach, colleague, friend, and model for all teachers; Sue Woodard, friend and gifted teacher of teachers; Ann Pavia for encouragement, tough questions, and more listening than anyone deserves; Dorothy Biggie, who modeled the power of the written word with her words and the power of faith with her life; Philippa Stratton, the editor who conceived this book, and whose persistence and magic made it a reality; my family, especially Bob, Pat, John, Brett, Bridget, and Bethany, who give time, support, love, and understanding—and gave so much more of it all to me during this project; and, finally, the children and parents of Trumansburg Elementary School, who humble and teach me every day as they lead with brilliant light.

1

~~~~~~~~~

"Feet First"
Into the World of Nonfiction

When Jimmy was in kindergarten, he wrote about a cow and then drew a picture of it (Figure 1.1). The spring before I met him, Jimmy's kindergarten teacher had told me that he lived on a working farm, and that this farm was very important to him. Large for his age, Jimmy was a shy child and a bit reluctant to speak, although well liked by the other children. His social interactions were characterized less by conversation than by actions and gestures. "Yep" and silence, his bright brown eyes darting from side to side, made up his repertory of responses. His journal entry on the first day of first grade included an initial consonant for *barn, silo, cat, pet, hamster,* and *grass* (Figure 1.2). By the following May, one of his journal entries was about the number of cows on his family's farm (Figure 1.3). It was his interest in cows that encouraged him to grow as a learner.

In the reader's workshop, Jimmy often spent time studying the farm page in *Richard Scarey's Best Word Book Ever* (1963). In individual conferences, he pointed to a label word, such as "corncrib" (p. 16), read it, and then added information from his own experience. In writer's workshop, the first piece he published was entitled "Chores":

I was sleeping. I had breakfast. I milked cows. I fed calves. I went home.

On a class trip to the library to check out books, he walked over to my side so that our arms touched, nudged me, and, still staring straight ahead, asked in his deep, raspy voice, "Where's the cow books?" Since I

~~~~~~~~~

Figure 1.1 *Jimmy's kindergarten story about the cows at his farm.*

was working with other children at the time, our librarian offered to help. She took his hand, explaining as they walked toward the book shelves, "Information books are kept over here."

The next time we were in the library, I began to tell the children how to find specific kinds of books. I wanted to give them information about how books were organized and arranged in the library and to foster an awareness of different kinds of writing. Remembering that Jimmy had found a book about cows (of course!), I decided to use his experience as an example. "Last week," I told the children, "Jimmy wanted to find books about cows and the librarian helped him find where information books—what we call nonfiction books—are shelved. When he looked there he found a book about cows. Jimmy, would you like to look for another one today?" He nodded. "Do you remember where to look?" He nodded. "Tell us, where did you find the book about cows?" I was expecting him to walk to the shelf and point. Instead, he handed me a scrap of paper on which he had written the call number! The librarian had mentioned the call number briefly as she guided him the previous week. Now,

Figure 1.2 *Jimmy's early first grade journal entry about his farm.*

although it is certainly within the capabilities of a first grader to write a note to himself, Jimmy's action was particularly significant. It demonstrated unusual maturity and sophistication, and indicated the power of his topic. When I thought about the experience later, I realized that following this narrow interest would enable Jimmy to expand his learning and grow in the school environment.

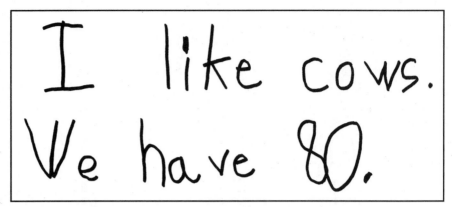

Figure 1.3 *Jimmy's later first grade journal entry.*

Like a drop of food coloring in a glass of water, Jimmy's interest in cows permeated his learning. One day, as I began reading *A Calf Is Born* (Kaizuki 1988) aloud to the class, he muttered, "It's a holstein." Later, as I turned to the page with the author's beautiful illustration of the birth, he whispered, "That's right. Feet first." His comment caught the attention of the group, and I stopped reading. As we looked at him, he put up his fore-arms and hands and said in a slightly louder voice, "*Feet* first." I nodded and read on while Jimmy smiled a satisfied smile.

Later in the year, he wrote a poem.

Cows
Cows can
Be black and cows can
Be brown and cows can
Be white and cows can
Be red and cows
Eat a lot of hay.

In his daily journal he wrote that he wanted to buy a Brown Swiss heifer calf and fill a silo by himself someday.

His last piece of the year was called "Dairy Cows." It included an illus-tration (Figure 1.4) and in general one sentence of text per page:

Dairy cows get milked 2 or 3 times a day. Cows milk is made out of grass because cows eat grass. Holsteins are black and white.

Figure 1.4 *"There are kinds of cows. Holsteins, Brown Swiss, Ayrshires, and jerseys."*

There are red and white holsteins too. Do cows have calves? Yes.
They are usually born frontwards. The mother usually licks the
calf. The calf usually walks. The cows eat lots. The cows eat corn
and wheat. They eat hay and they drink water. There are kinds of
cows. Holsteins, Brown Swiss, Ayrshires, jerseys. Mastitis is a dis-
ease for cows. Part 2 of Dairy Cows. Cows have number names.
Part 3 of Dairy Cows. Dairy cows are milked in a parlor.

Three years later, when my current first-grade class was planning a
trip to the dairy farm at Cornell University, I thought of Jimmy (trans-
formed to Jimbo in third grade and to James in fourth), and invited him
back to his former classroom to share his expertise. He agreed reluctant-
ly and when he appeared, spoke briefly. Afterwards, when he invited questions, however, his answers were wonderful! He beamed with pride and
pleasure, and even managed a response to the question, "How do you tell
the boy cows from the girl cows?"

Later that day, I saw him on the playground and thanked him for visiting the class. Then I asked him a question I routinely ask my former students, "What are you reading?"

"Oh, a farming manual...I can't remember the name...but it tells about free-stall barns," he replied, swinging one leg and looking at the ground. "Free-stall barns...well...."

When Jimmy entered his first-grade classroom, he discovered a whole new world, as do most children in a new classroom. The teacher determines needs and gathers materials, but what is perhaps more important, she encourages children to "notice," "invent," "discover," "wonder," "consider," and "dream" as they explore. I like to invite young children to join Frank Smith's (1986) "Literacy Club," to sit around Nancie Atwell's (1987) dining room table, to work and play, in other words, in a place where reading and writing pervade the environment. Like seedlings pushing up toward the sun in a spring garden, the children delight in the height and breadth of their literacy: they reach, change, and grow. The classroom environment can provide a safe place for learning and laughter, help from adults and peers, and stimulating materials, but the key lies within the individual child. Curiosity, interest and enthusiasm, and a deep need to know are what create "a learner" and build a foundation for nonfiction literacy.

The Russian theorist L. S. Vygotsky (1978), writing in the 1930s, helped us understand how children learn. Vygotsky recognized that language, social interaction, and environment are components of what he called the "zone of proximal development." Within that zone, the child learns and grows. Jimmy's literacy was based on—and flourished in—nonfiction. His best work, the times he stretched and grew most as a reader and writer, focused on what he knew and loved: farming. Of course, there is nothing new about finding the right topic or the right book for a particular child. In Jimmy's case, however, respecting his passion for farming had a powerful influence on his literacy. It underscored and encouraged his connection to the literate community.

It is fiction, however, that seems to form the primary path of early literacy. The Caldecott Medal offers a telling example. This prestigious annual award, named for the nineteenth-century illustrator Randolph Caldecott, honors the illustrator of the year's most distinguished American picture book for children. Yet fifty-four of the fifty-eight medals awarded to date (93 percent) have recognized fiction or folk tale selections. I would estimate that in the past, the ratio of fiction to nonfiction in the primary classroom has been similarly uneven. Nonfiction in primary-grade language arts is too often the exception. Early literacy learning has been based in fiction, whether the child prefers nonfiction or not.

Are we to assume that young children cannot be motivated to read nonfiction? If not, then why has quality nonfiction for these young readers lagged behind quality fiction? And what happens to the child who is drawn to nonfiction?

In recent years, writers, illustrators, and publishers have produced a wealth of inviting nonfiction for primary-age children. Today, nonavailability is no longer an excuse for neglect. And more available genres mean more engaged readers and writers like Jimmy. Primary teachers want to encourage the literacy of the children in their classrooms, and nonfiction is an essential part of that experience. Language arts genre selection in the primary grades needs to broaden, and that is the focus of this book.

Of course, introducing nonfiction in the primary classroom is not a new idea. But as I discovered, simply making books available and reading them aloud when they supported a particular content area in the curriculum was not enough. The children did not experience the richness of the genre. I decided to search for ways to make nonfiction a more important presence in my classroom.

2

~~~~~~~~~~~~~~~~

"Michael Put His Rubber Snake
with the Reptile Books"
180 Days of Nonfiction

August 15

Dear First Grader,

Room 7 has been cleaned and I am beginning to get things ready for September 5. That's the day you will come to school, and I can't wait!

I've been reading words on packages and signs, and I was wondering if you have a package or sign with a word on it that you can read. It might be on a box or a bag of food or on a toy. It might be in the newspaper. If you can, please bring the word with you so that we can put it on our bulletin board. Then, you can teach everyone in Room 7 to read your word!

I would also like you to bring a shoebox to school with your name on the side of the box where the shoe size is found. Please put two or three things in the box that will remind you to tell us something about yourself. You might choose a picture of your family, a part of a favorite toy, your favorite book, or whatever you would like. We will call it your "Me Box" and we will use it to get to know each other.

You will also need sneakers for gym and a paint smock for art…

Before the school year begins, each child receives a letter like this one describing the first two "nonfiction" activities of the year. On the bulletin board we will display the words the children have discovered in the envi-

~~~~~

ronment around them. For some children, these information words—proper nouns and directions—will be the first words they read. The second activity, the "Me Box," is the beginning of the child's portfolio, which I will discuss in more detail later. After the children have shared the contents of their boxes with all of us, each item becomes an "artifact": the child draws it on a piece of paper, or we make a photocopy, and this record goes into the child's portfolio. The portfolio represents the child's development as a person and a learner and documents his or her individual growth. The portfolio itself becomes a collection of nonfiction, a gathering together of information we will be able to use in assessment and setting goals.

Before I wrote my letter of welcome, I had already decided to make nonfiction an equal partner in the language arts curriculum. First I established a working definition in my own mind: Nonfiction is a literary genre whose primary purpose is to inform or persuade. Because nonfiction literacy builds on the literate encounters children have experienced long before they enter school, I also decided to incorporate nonfiction into the everyday routines and experiences of our classroom. Beginning the very first day, the environment, the atmosphere, and the learning materials would demonstrate that nonfiction forms a huge piece of the literacy pie.

Listening and Speaking

Bursting with excitement, Lisa shared her news. "You know my cat, Siesta? Well, she had her kittens! She had five and we are not sure how many are girls and how many are boys." A small group gathered around her.

"Are any of them dead? Because when my cat had kittens, some died."

"No! They are all alive and Siesta is licking them to keep them clean and they are drinking her milk."

"Did you watch them when they were borned?"

"I was outside and my mom called me in and there were already two but I saw the rest when they first came out."

"How did they look when they first came out?"

"Icky! They were bloody but Siesta cleaned them. She licked them."

"OOOOugh!"

"Are you going to keep any of them?"

"My mom says we have to find people who want a kitten when they are older but now they have to stay with us. They all have to stay with Siesta and drink her milk. I'm going to ask if I can keep one."

"What color are they?"

While this discussion continued, I located Joanna Cole's *My New Kitten* (1995). "Should I use it for a read-aloud," I wondered, "or give it to Lisa during reading workshop?" Then I realized that I was not a key player in the learning that was going on in Lisa's group; the children were doing just fine on their own! So I listened and observed and eventually passed the book on to Lisa during reading workshop. She took it eagerly and shared it with the whole group at the end of the workshop, supplementing each page of text by noting any similarities and differences in her own experience.

Young children love to talk, and much of what they know they have learned by listening to other children and to adults. Speech and information are natural allies. A nonfiction read-aloud to the whole group, for example, encourages conversation, a crucial part of nonfiction literacy. As Sylvia Vardell and Kathleen Copeland (1992) observe, "Read Aloud time with nonfiction often becomes spontaneously interactive. Questions arise, experiences are remembered, responses are shared, discussion occurs. Half the reading time may be spent talking about this new information. But this is a great gift of the genre—to develop critical thinking so that students become more active in their processing of information and less accepting of the text as the final word" (p. 85). Nonfiction is embedded in the activities of the classroom.

Formerly, the teacher did most of the speaking and the students most of the listening. In today's classrooms, this trend has been reversed, and "spontaneous interaction" has had a positive effect. In current thinking about language instruction there is consensus: the teacher's role is to do more and better listening, and children's to engage in more talk about their thinking and learning. This kind of engagement in listening and speaking should not be underestimated. It is a cornerstone of nonfiction literacy growth.

The Classroom Library

In our classroom, books are everywhere (the floor plan is shown in Figure 2.1). They are organized conveniently so that children will use them fre-

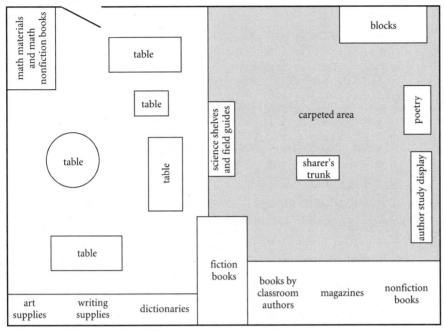

Figure 2.1 *Classroom floor plan.*

quently and successfully. This "user friendly" system, already in place on the first day of school, remains consistent throughout the year and parallels that of the school library. At one time or another, the children have offered revealing comments about the books in the classroom library:

> "This book needs a dot."
> "I think this book belongs in nonfiction, not poetry!"
> "I don't know what to read today…I guess I'll go look at dinosaur books."
> "Who's got the insect field guide?"
> "Let's make a basket of frog books and put it next to the tadpoles."
> "Fiction is a mess! I'll straighten it."
> "This book was in with 'animals' but I'm gonna move it to 'pets' because it is about a dog and a dog is a pet."
> "This book about wolves has a werewolf in it. Werewolves aren't real so I don't think this book should be with nonfiction."
> "We need more books about gerbils."
> "I put *Hats Hats Hats* (Morris 1989) in with 'clothes' yesterday and now it's gone."

"Mrs. Duthie, Michael put his rubber snake in the reptile books!"

"All the books on airplanes are too hard for me, and I want to read about airplanes."

"Let's take the bird books and read them under the table so no one bothers us."

"I'm going to keep working on *Your Big Backyard*."

I use circle stickers in different colors to identify which genre each book belongs to (green for nonfiction, brown for fiction, and so on) and house each genre on separate, labeled bookshelves. In this way, long before children refer to a literary genre in speaking they understand the underlying logic and purpose of this method of organizing. This understanding guides them in selecting books as early as the first week of school.

The classroom library is organized according to genre for several reasons:

- to help children locate books on their own
- to assist children in finding a book for "spontaneous investigation"
- to demonstrate similarities and differences between books
- to parallel the organization of the school library
- to help young readers distinguish between genres
- to promote critical thinking

In addition, arranging books by topic within genres gives individual nonfiction titles added power: four books on a single topic grouped together on the same shelf seem to gain significance. For example, an older book about caring for a pet has less appeal when it is randomly mixed in with fiction and other nonfiction than when it is one title among a larger collection of books on pets. A child committed to a certain topic is more apt to read all the available books on that topic if they are housed side by side. At the same time, this arrangement allows children to compare information in one book with that in another book on the same topic. When they wonder about the differences, they often come up with reasons to explain them, which promotes critical thinking. The simple contrast in the appearance of older books and newer books on the same topic suggests that information changes and new information becomes available. It also demonstrates that there are many ways to write about the same topic and that nonfiction writers choose different approaches, some more effective than others.

Every year, a child brings me a book, such as Jack Prelutsky's poetry anthology *Tyrannosaurus Was a Beast* (1988), and tells me we should change the color of dot that indicates its genre. When I ask why, the child usually explains that this book gives information, so it should be with nonfiction, not poetry. I encourage the child to change the dot. But then, before too long, the same book finds its way into the hands of another child, who reverses the process. If a class discussion results, we explore both points of view. Did the author write this book to give us information? Was the author trying to teach us about something or tell us a make-believe story? Which was most important to the author? Using these criteria, the children considered and easily placed Joanna Cole's *The Magic School Bus Lost in the Solar System* (1990) with nonfiction books about space, because, we concluded, Joanna Cole wrote this book to teach us about space.

Year-Round Author Study

On the first day of school I initiate an author study. As a group, we review all of a particular author's work, or a selection, in order to become familiar with the author's writing style and subject matter, and the literary genre he or she seems to prefer. I usually begin with fiction, the kind of writing most familiar to young children, and, more than likely, I begin with the work of Frank Asch. In *Happy Birthday, Moon* (1982), Bear thinks he is talking to the moon when he is really responding to his own echo, while in *Bear Shadow* (1985) Bear tries to change the position of his shadow because it interferes with his fishing. After about a week of reading Asch's books in read-alouds and, in some cases, on their own, the children conclude that he writes make-believe stories, often about bears who act erroneously because they misunderstand scientific phenomena. (Later in the year they will discover Frank Asch's poetry and nonfiction.)

I usually follow the Asch study with the work of a nonfiction author like Anne Rockwell. I include *Our Yard Is Full of Birds* (1992a), *What We Like* (1992b), *Bear Child's Book of Special Days* (1989b), and *Apples and Pumpkins* (1989a), among others, in the study. The children quickly notice that she is not writing make-believe stories. As one child observed, "Anne Rockwell tells us about stuff. Like…she picks out something and then tells us all about it." As we read more authors and talk about how they differ in style and subject matter, children's literacy expands. They become more aware of genre, and they begin to associate specific authors with specific characteristics.

Later in the year, we read books by Gail Gibbons, a nonfiction author who has written many books on a wide variety of topics. Her engaging illustrations and text immediately capture the interest of young children. At this point I begin to encourage more detailed discussion of how an author presents information than I have earlier in the year. As a writer, Gail Gibbons clearly complies with Jean Fritz's (1988) characterizations: "The art of fiction is making up facts; the art of nonfiction is using facts to make up form" (p. 759).

As I read Gail Gibbons's books aloud each day over a week or so, we discover new delights: her clever delivery of "how-to" information in *The Pottery Place* (1987), the whale facts chart in *Whales* (1991c), the story she tells in *The Puffins Are Back* (1991b) to teach us about those wonderful birds, and her clearly labeled drawings in *From Seed to Plant* (1991a). We also notice that some of her books contain much more print than others, and that she often surprises us with new information about familiar things. Now I begin to focus the mini-lessons on specific aspects of nonfiction. We look at Gail Gibbons's use of particular elements and begin making a list, which we will discuss and then post for future reference.

During free-choice time, I have observed children making pots of coiled clay with *The Pottery Place* propped up nearby for reference, or whale skeletons out of toothpicks and macaroni following Gibbons's labeled drawing in *Whales*. I delight in children's initiative when they experiment using a text as a guide. In a slightly different kind of "text involvement," a child once returned a Gibbons book to the library along with a check. "My dog chewed it," she explained. The other children collapsed in giggles because the book was *Say Woof: The Day of a Country Veterinarian* (1992a). "I guess your dog doesn't like vets!" they teased.

I am convinced that these author studies, carried out routinely throughout the school year, help to broaden children's understanding of literature. Children begin to view authors as real people like themselves, to investigate a variety of topics, and to think more critically. Patrick's comment on Donald Crews's work illustrates the last point: "I think he could use a little more words on each page. He does good pictures but he doesn't use enough words."

Consistent exposure to nonfiction as a basic part of their literate experience encourages children to choose nonfiction books on their own. As readers, they notice that each author writes in a distinctive way. Author studies in various genres not only reinforce this idea, they also introduce children to the notion of "voice" in writing, which can be a powerful insight. Children discover that writers present information in a personal style and with a particular point of view. When young readers come across conflicting information in different sources, they begin to see the need to consider and evaluate it critically. At the same time, the author's personal voice invites them to delve further into the subject. When this author invitation intersects with reader curiosity, together they form a dynamic partnership for learning. In nurturing curiosity in the classroom, the teacher can capitalize on this match by extending children's exploration to all areas of the curriculum.

Along with Gail Gibbons, a number of other nonfiction writers have proven effective in author studies with primary children. They include

Byron Barton
Melvin Berger (Macmillan Big Books)
Joanna Cole
Donald Crews
Tomie de Paola
Arthur Dorros
David Drew (Rigby Big Books)
Dick Gackenback
Rita Golden Gelman
William T. and Lindsay George
Gail Gibbons
Rosmarie Hausherr
Ron Hirschi
Patricia Lauber
Bruce MacMillan
Betsy Maestro
Ann Morris
Ken Robbins
Anne Rockwell
Joanne Ryder
Millicent Selsam

Of course, I could never include all these authors during any one school year. Instead, I choose from the list according to the particular interests of my students and the availability of books, looking at some writers for a few days and at others for a week or more.

Throughout the year, when children refer to books in science, social studies, and other content areas written by an author we have studied, they are able to examine the author's style more closely because they are already familiar with the author's work. As writers, children are tempted to apply what they have learned about style and genre to their own writing. Jake, for example, wrote a piece he entitled "How Incredible Ice Cream Is Made," which he dedicated "to Melvin Berger whose books helped me make this story." Children copy the unique "language" of nonfiction, and their familiarity with individual authors helps them to do it.

Writing Workshop

During writing workshop the children color code the cover sheet of their drafts (Figure 2.2), using a system modeled after the class library color coding. This effectively focuses their awareness on genre in their own writing and supports the reading-writing connection. Children generally choose their own topic and genre, and in this way discover which genres are most effective for their topics. The color code also helps children locate a specific item in their writing folder more quickly and identify an item by genre in cases when more than one piece is in progress. I once overheard a child say, "Should I work on tan or green, my fiction or nonfiction writing today…the monster or the raccoon?" When I confer with children about their writing, the color code provides immediate information. "I see this is coded as nonfiction so I know that you are giving information. Let's see how you've chosen to do it." (Chapter 4 will address nonfiction writing workshop and the nonfiction genre study in more detail.)

In our classroom, we "celebrate" each published piece: the writer gives a reading to the whole group and receives their applause. At this point I ask the child, "Is this your best piece of nonfiction? If you decide that it is, put it in your portfolio." Children's participation in this decision encourages self-evaluation and highlights genre issues.

```
┌─────────────────────────────────────────────────┐
│ (staple)                                          │
│                          (What kind of writing is it?) │
│                              (brown for fiction)  │
│                              (green for nonfiction)│
│                              (red for poetry)     │
│                                                   │
│  Date: _____                               │
│                                                   │
│  Title:                                           │
│                                                   │
│                                                   │
│                                                   │
│  Author:_____                               │
│                                                   │
│                                                   │
│              I read this to myself._____        │
│                                                   │
│              I read this to_____          │
└─────────────────────────────────────────────────┘
```

Figure 2.2 *Color-coded cover sheet for children's writing drafts.*

Content Areas

One year, my class was chosen to play the dragon in our school Dragon Parade celebrating Chinese New Year. After the parade, we "feasted" on Chinese dishes using chopsticks. For some children, it was a new—and difficult—way to eat. They commented on logistical difficulties; estimated how much food had been eaten, dropped, and left on the plate; tallied their success and failure; and compared our day to that of Ernie Wan in *Lion Dancer: Ernie Wan's Chinese New Year* (Waters 1990). Those who were adept with chopsticks helped those who were not. Some devised better eating methods and others speculated about the feasibility of using chopsticks to eat other foods (such as hamburgers, pizza, and grapes). The following day, one child reported on the experience of eating with chopsticks in his journal (Figure 2.3): "You put your middle finger in the middle and your thumb on the bottom and your other three at the top and push with the other three!"

Was this a science lesson on levers? A social studies exploration of cultural customs? An exercise to foster self-esteem? An example of cooperative learning or critical thinking? A display of small muscle coordination? A math adventure in estimating, counting, or tallying? A nonfiction

Figure 2.3 *A journal entry on eating with chopsticks.*

reading-related encounter? An exercise in how to write directions? It was all of these and more, a direct result of the habits, skills, and attitudes of the learners engaged in an open-ended learning opportunity.

In *Science Workshop: A Whole Language Approach* (1993), Wendy Saul characterizes science as "a way of thinking, a way of viewing the world, an approach to problem solving" (p. 4). I would add that for "science" we could just as legitimately substitute mathematics, social studies, or reading and writing. It is not surprising, therefore, that these disciplinary "curricula" function in similar ways within a community of learners and thinkers. They not only engage young learners in a specific discipline for the sake of the learning and enjoyment, they also offer an opportunity to explore, predict, speculate, hypothesize, estimate, and investigate. Children can practice

- identifying a specific problem
- reviewing their prior knowledge
- deciding which aspects of a problem or situation are important
- determining their audience
- determining their focus
- gathering data
- recording observations
- sorting and classifying information
- sharing personal and group investigations
- calculating
- using graphs, drawings, and other forms of visual representation
- seeking multiple solutions
- respecting different points of view
- forming opinions
- sharing information and concerns
- asking pertinent questions
- analyzing
- considering likenesses and differences
- examining parts of a whole
- summarizing and assessing
- drawing conclusions
- setting goals
- reading and writing

Nonfiction literacy is supported by the same skills, habits, attitudes, and processes inherent in the approach of the scientist, mathematician, and social scientist and is reinforced by classroom activities designed to promote thinking and learning in these fields. During explorations within these disciplines, the teacher can be on the lookout for opportune moments to point out the significant role of nonfiction literacy:

Where did you find that out?
Who remembers where we read that?

I read, in this book, something a little different.
Would you draw that so we can keep track of changes?
Where could we find out more about…?
Let's keep a list of…
Cal, do you still have that book that told about…?
Who will write that down for us so we remember?
What kind of graph could we make to…?
Who remembers the call number for books about…?
Remember Jamal's brother's book? How did it…?
Let's look for that next time we're in the library.
I wonder if the illustration in Gail Gibbons's book shows that?

Comments and questions like these, at the "teachable moment," encourage awareness and independent thinking.

Environmental Print

Children encounter environmental print at the beginning of the school year, when they bring words in to teach to the group and post on the classroom bulletin board. As the year progresses, it becomes an even more complex source of information. "What are we going to do?" someone asked. We had already planted sunflowers outside our classroom window when the children made a startling discovery: since our classroom was close to the playground, stray balls and running feet trampled some of the seedlings! The children suggested several plans of action. One was to make signs ("Please be careful"; "No balls!"; "Don't walk here!"; "No running here"; "Plants growing") and tape them to the windows above the plants with the message and illustration facing out (see Figure 2.4). With their signs, the children communicated information that was important to them. (Ultimately, they succeeded in saving the sunflower seedlings from feet and playground balls but not in seeing them grow and mature: they were accidentally cut down with the grass by hurried custodial personnel!)

One spring, a six-year-old boy with freckles and red hair, whose mother had cut his hair outdoors to avoid a messy cleanup indoors, brought in a bird nest that had fallen from a tree near his home. It was lined with red hair! He displayed the nest in the classroom with a sign that read "Birds recycle too!"

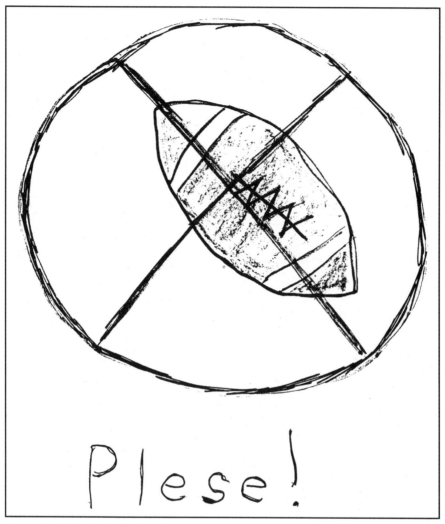

Figure 2.4 *"No football, please!"*

Children see environmental print everywhere around them, but in the primary classroom it serves to bridge the gap between the real world and the print world. Tailored to a narrow age group, it gains in power by its relevance to a particular subject. It also models various nonfiction techniques, such as writing directions, captioning, and labeling. The signs and labels are functional and useful, enabling young learners to work with more efficiency, enjoyment, and understanding. And since environmental print supplies information, it can be considered nonfiction!

Portfolios

One February the children were eager to take home their portfolios, which had "grown" from their August "Me Box." Jenna was excited about the portfolio. She kept hers current, making changes and additions throughout the year to reflect herself as a person and to demonstrate how she had grown as a learner. Her portfolio contained a drawing of the South Korean flag as an artifact of the country where she was born, a photocopy of her Walkman to represent her interest in music, and her best piece of writing and handwriting—an autobiography. Tucked into the pocket of the folder was an audiotape of her oral reading samples, along with other documentation.

Jenna bounced into the classroom one day and announced, "Today's the day! My mom and dad can't wait. I can't wait!" She was more excited than she was on her birthday. She had already shared her portfolio with several classmates, her fourth-grade Reading Partner, and me. She had returned the "appointment sheet" from home verifying that her parents had set aside time for Jenna to present her portfolio to them. During the morning, she told me that she had one more thing to put into her portfolio and added a colorful sheet, decorated with shooting stars, that said, "Dear Mom and Dad. I couldn't wait and tell you about my portfolio. I love you. From Jenna" (see Figure 2.5). When three o'clock finally arrived, she packed the portfolio in a large manila envelope and patted the bulge, giggling with excitement. She knew its contents would be received by an eager, appreciative audience.

The next day, when Jenna brought her portfolio back, she reported on the pleasure she and her family had experienced. She shared her parents' comments on her presentation and proudly filed them away in her portfolio, but then quickly reopened it: "Oh, good!" she said, "They remembered to put the date on the comments." Jenna had learned that information like this is often more valuable when dated. She stowed her portfolio in the storage basket, ready for a new day and new discoveries.

Portfolios become a kind of continuous autobiography, since they reflect children's growth in many areas. Jenna's included items relevant to literacy, including nonfiction literacy, and was itself a piece of nonfiction. She continually added new items and reconsidered earlier ones, replacing some in order to keep her portfolio current.

In guiding children as they create their portfolios, I suggest that they include a number of different nonfiction items, for example:

Figure 2.5 *Jenna's portfolio letter to her parents.*

a piece of nonfiction writing the child deems her best with an explanation of why she considers it better than previous writing or what it reveals about her. One boy included a piece about a natural disaster in his portfolio "because I told about the flood at the lake so we would remember how it happened, so next time it happens, we will get our boat out of the water before it sinks." He judged his record of the incident significant enough to qualify it as his best nonfiction writing.

a current genre chart listing the child's dominant weekly reading choice in either fiction, nonfiction, or poetry.

a list of book call numbers on subjects of interest (Figure 2.6). It is not unusual for a child to consult the list before heading out to the school library. The child updates the list, adding other call numbers as his areas of interest change or expand.

a copy of the child's self-evaluation graph, which I include in my quarterly reports to parents throughout the year on various topics.

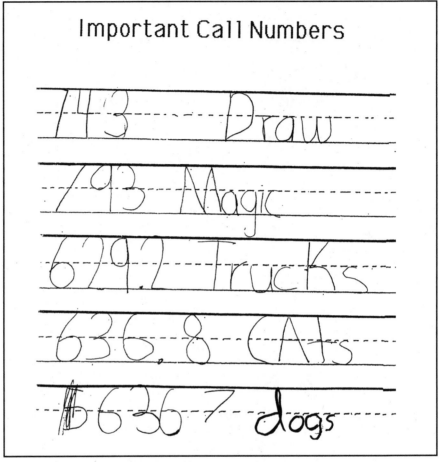

Figure 2.6 *A child's personal list of library call numbers.*

Does Jimmy's evaluation of his own writing (Figure 2.7) match the picture of him as a writer presented in Chapter 1?

entries from their science or math journals (Figures 2.8 and 2.9) that document their research as scientists and mathematicians, or from their personal journals (Figure 2.10). As I conferred with Alex about this entry, he told me, "This is biography writing."

an audiotape of the child's oral reading samples over the school year. In making her selections for this tape, the child is encouraged to choose readings from several genres, including nonfiction, that illustrate her growth as a reader. The tape demonstrates the child's

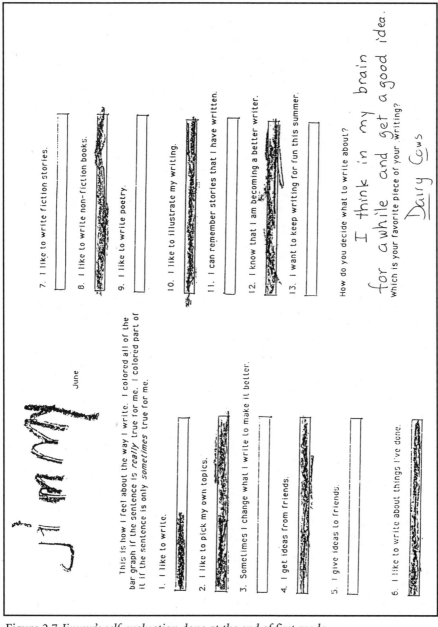

Figure 2.7 *Jimmy's self-evaluation done at the end of first grade.*

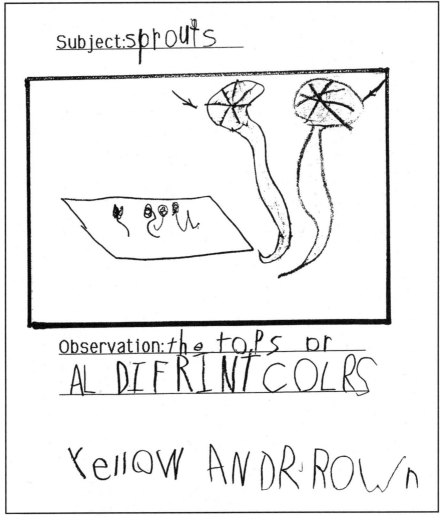

Figure 2.8 *A child's science journal entry.*

fluency in reading increasingly difficult texts and compares her oral reading ability in one genre with that in another genre.

In reading nonfiction, children are more likely than in other genres to interact verbally with the text:

"Oh, yeah, I see it in the picture."
"I wonder if all birds do that."
"That's not what the other book said."

the APOLLS SILL WAY
the SAM AS 5 UOON
VOONAFIX KUBS!

Figure 2.9 *"The apples still weigh the same as 5 unifix cubes!": a math journal entry.*

Because the tape also captures these mumbled comments, it offers additional insights into the child's involvement in the text and his nonfiction literacy.

Nonfiction encourages a broad view of the world and its people. Because young children are especially fascinated by the world and want to find out more about it, the primary grades are an ideal time to introduce nonfiction. In her book *The Sense of Wonder* (1956), the naturalist Rachel Carson writes, "If a child is to keep alive his inborn sense of wonder...he needs the companionship of at least one adult who can share it, rediscovering with him the joy, excitement and mystery of the world we live in" (p. 45). In the classroom, that adult is the teacher.

"What are you reading?" and "What are you writing?" are questions I routinely ask my former students in casual conversation. But their responses often have an air of seriousness about them as they tell me about nonfiction; required reading, research for reports, and group pro-

Figure 2.10 *"On New Year's Eve I stayed up to 12 at night!": a personal journal entry.*

jects. Few of them speak positively or enthusiastically about reading or writing nonfiction. I wondered: Do primary teachers help children realize that nonfiction is a significant literary genre woven into our daily lives in many ways? Is too much language arts time in the primary classroom spent in genres other than nonfiction? Are young learners too unfamiliar with the unique aspects of the genre to find it interesting or pleasurable? I decided to reapportion the time I devoted to various genres in my classroom. When I looked at children, classroom routines, curriculum, environment—and my own attitude—I found plenty of reasons and ways to make changes.

- Reading and writing nonfiction in content areas is not enough.
- Nonfiction author studies are not enough.
- Simply having nonfiction books available in the classroom is not enough.
- "Waiting until third grade" is a poor option.

- Nonfiction needs a proper introduction if it is to become a lifelong "friend."
- Young readers need nonfiction as they grow in literacy.

We don't have to trick children or force them to become enthusiastic about nonfiction. Effective attitudes, routines, habits, and environments can transform children's experience of nonfiction into an exciting journey of discovery, guided, as Rachel Carson says, by an "inborn sense of wonder."

3

~~~~~~~~~~

"I Never Knew that Horses
Could Wear Armor"
Nonfiction Reading Workshop

"The feel of the water, its gentle laughter, and the smell of the bog just upstream. They all said one thing, 'Welcome home, little brother'" (p. 29). I closed *Little Brother Moose* (Kasperson 1995) and stood it on the trunk next to me. The classroom was unusually quiet for a few moments.

Then someone said, "I wonder why a moose got so mixed up?"

"It's because people got him mixed up but then something else could happen; then he could die."

"'Cause he didn't have food."

"That happens to other animals too, like lions in Africa and bears."

"Sometimes people shoot the animal and it's not fair."

"Sometimes people don't shoot the animals when they go where people live. They catch them and put them in a cage and take them to where they want the animals to live."

"But I think mostly, they shoot them."

After a few minutes, I asked, "Was this book nonfiction?" The six- and seven-year-olds paused again, until finally one child ventured, "Yes and no both."

"What do you mean yes *and* no?"

"Yes because we were learning about what happens to a moose when people move real close up to where he lives. But it's no too because I don't think Little Brother Moose is real."

This comment led into a brief mini-lesson. "The author wanted to teach us about the moose and decided that it would be a good idea to tell

~~~~~~~

us the information in a story. You know that it is the job of the author to decide how to write so that the readers will understand what the author wants to tell. I think James Kasperson wanted to help the moose, and he thought that if he told about what happened to one moose, his readers might understand better. You were just talking about exactly that and I think that, if he were listening to you James Kasperson would say that his story worked. He would be glad that he gave you information so you would understand the moose's problem. That's what nonfiction authors do. They give information."

This conversation occurred during a nonfiction reading workshop in a first-grade classroom. After the mini-lesson, the children scattered around the room to their favorite places. Anna and Kevin hurried to the corner behind the Big Book stand with *Sunflower* (Ford 1995) to discuss the seed placement "like a round pattern" in the flower's center. Lee perched on the stool with *Manatees* (Cousteau Society 1992), carefully examining the photographs of this clumsy looking animal as a graceful swimmer. Lisa and Allison scanned the table of contents in *Glove, Mitten, and Sock Puppets* (Gates 1978) and made plans for free-choice time later that morning.

I grabbed my clipboard and stopped at Andrew's table. Andrew was rereading the pronunciation of "Diplodocus" in Peggy Parish's *Dinosaur Time* (1974). "I used to think this part [pointing to the pronunciation guide embedded in the text] was the dinosaurs' other name, but now I know it helps me to say the regular name. It doesn't really help me now because I already know how to say it, but I like to read it anyway."

"Does it help you in other books when you don't know how to say the word?" I asked.

"Yeah, a little. But it helps my mom a lot more cause she doesn't know very much about nature and stuff. Like…one time my mom was reading me this book about the ocean that Grant, like, found for me in the library, and she couldn't read some of the names of the plants and fish so, like, I told her to use it. But in that book we had to look in the back to find out how to say it. Another book we had didn't have a page to tell you how to say the hard words so we, I mean my mom, like, just guessed."

"So, you know where you can find help to say the hard words in some books?"

"Yep. But sometimes, like, if the book doesn't tell you, then it's okay to just guess, like my mom did," and he turned back to *Dinosaur Time*.

Next I stopped with Amy and Wendy, who each had a copy of Byron Barton's *Building a House* (1981) and were taking turns reading it.

"They are building a garage near my house and I saw them do some of this stuff like pour cement. It was cool because the boards on the sides made it all stay inside and when they took the boards off, the cement was hard as a rock. They spilt a little cement on the ground outside where the boards were and when it dried it wasn't connected to the rest of the garage floor."

"I didn't know that they use boards to hold the cement together until it gets hard. That's a good idea."

"Yeah, so it doesn't leak out."

"I can see the boards right here in the picture." Amy traced her finger around the frame in the illustration. "Did you touch the wet cement near your house?"

"No."

"Then how do you know it was hard?"

"Because I saw people walking on it another day!"

"Know what? One time…a long time ago last year…my big brother …wrote his name in cement that was wet. It was on a sidewalk…he got in trouble…he got grounded when my mom saw it…and his name is *still* in the cement and he didn't even write it very good! My mom says she gets mad every time she sees it."

On my clipboard I noted that the girls were relating their nonfiction reading to events in their own lives.

I moved on to Robert, who was struggling as he attempted to read Joanna Cole's *My New Kitten* (1995). As I sat down, Robert said, "See this kitten? It looks almost just like mine. You know, the one I got with my grandpa."

"Oh, I remember. You and your grandpa found it and couldn't find the owner, right?"

"Yeah."

"Is this book helping you to learn more about your kitten?" Robert's smile faded.

"No, not really, 'cause it's too hard."

"Where could you look for another book about cats that would be just right for you to read?"

"With the pet books."

"Do you need help?"

"Nope."

Later, during reading workshop, I found Robert laughing at the antics of Jack in *My Cat Jack* (Casey 1994), and during writing workshop, flipping through both books before he began to write.

Genre Study Within the Reading Workshop

These encounters took place during the nonfiction genre study, which *replaces* our year-long author study format (see Chapter 2) for a period of two to four weeks, and includes nonfiction read-alouds and mini-lessons in both the reading and writing workshops. The goal of the nonfiction genre study is to expand children's exposure to the elements of nonfiction and to encourage familiarity and enjoyment. It builds on and enriches previous nonfiction experiences by allowing children to choose topics and investigate new information while drawing on what they already know.

The nonfiction genre study, grounded in a literate, learning environment, capitalizes on the child's natural need to explore. Like all learning in the primary classroom, the nonfiction genre study supports and guides the learner at a crucial time in the formation of lifelong literacy habits.

The reading workshop in our first-grade classroom, modeled on the work of many, was initially inspired and shaped by Jane Hansen's *When Writers Read* (1987). Throughout the year, the reading workshop generally followed the same format:

- a read-aloud of a piece by the author we are currently studying, and questions and comments from the group.
- a thirty-minute block of independent reading in self-selected books and direct documentation (Johnston 1992, 1993a), including individual and small-group conferences with the teacher.
- a "Book Talk" within the independent reading period (described later in this chapter).
- a whole-group share led by two children, who, after a brief introduction, read a book (or part of one) and then take questions and comments from the group. In addition, the teacher gives the child a family note (see Figure 3.1) in celebration of the share.

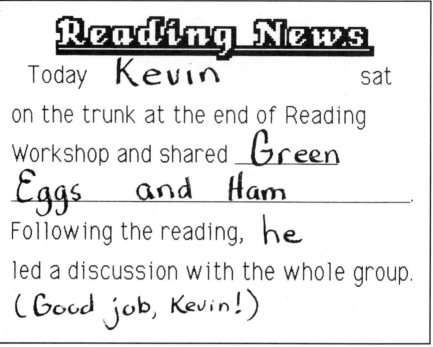

Figure 3.1 *A family note to celebrate Kevin's whole-group reading share.*

I based my approach to nonfiction genre study on my earlier experience with poetry. I had found that focusing on a single genre in reading and writing for a finite period of time with the entire class was beneficial and resulted in long-term payoffs. It heightened awareness and established common ground for large and small group conferences and mini-lessons (Duthie and Zimet 1993). It seemed to me that this same approach could benefit nonfiction literacy.

Get Set

I make it a habit to scour monthly primary book club lists, garage sales, and library discard shelves for nonfiction books. My classroom thus has a core collection of old, "loved" books, but many of them are held together by staples and tape. Although not essential, it is helpful to offer the children bright, "new-to-the-classroom" nonfiction books to highlight the genre. So I go to the school and the public libraries to acquire a nonfiction collection that caters to the interests of the children in a particular class. My aim is to create a nonfiction collection that is varied in topic and style.

The "new" books are sorted according to the general topics established at the beginning of the school year, which efficiently serve young children as they organize, classify, and locate titles. The specific categories themselves are less important than the fact that they suit the children's needs and interests. The nonfiction topics in our classroom include

alphabet
American Sign Language
animals that live in or near
   water
biographies
birds
clothes
colors
dinosaurs
farm animals
food
how-to-make (including
   recipes)
insects
jobs
machines

magazines
music
newspapers
numbers
our bodies
pets
places
plants
reptiles
rocks
seasons
space
sports
water
wild animals

We're Off!

When we begin the nonfiction genre study, instead of concentrating on one book or one author I introduce several books and several authors. The contrasts in style and presentation illustrate the idea that there is more than one possible approach. Readers can ask themselves which presentation was most effective and why. For each contrast reading mini-lesson, I try to include a familiar book from an earlier author study or one we have read earlier in the year in a content area. I select books for the daily mini-lessons on a wide range of subjects to involve the maximum number of students and keep interest high. I also try to use old and new paperback and hardcover books in order to reinforce the adage "You can't judge a book by its cover." Generally, I do not read all of the books aloud during the mini-lesson, but I might read one completely and then browse through the others, reading some sections and pointing out similarities and differences in information and presentation. Another day I might read two and browse through one.

Each year I select different books for the nonfiction genre study mini-lessons on contrast. One year, the topics for the first week included trucks, whales, how-to books, our bodies, and musical instruments.

Monday
Books:
> Aladdin Books, *Eye Openers: Trucks* (1991)
> Donald Crews, *Trucks* (1980)
> Gail Gibbons, *Trucks* (1981)

Mini-lesson:
> "How are these books organized?"

Main nonfiction characteristic:
> organized by
> > • function
> > • movement
> > • differences in physical parts

Tuesday
Books:
> Gail Gibbons, *Whales* (1991c)
> Louise Martin, *Whales* (1988)
> Seymour Simon, *Whales* (1989)

Mini-lesson:
> "What kind of pictures did the authors use?"

Main nonfiction characteristics:
> use of photographs vs. use of drawings
> labeling

Additional characteristics:
> > • index
> > • tables

Wednesday
Books:
> Clare Beaton, *Face Painting* (1990)
> Tomie de Paola, *Things to Make and Do on Valentine's Day* (1976)

Morteza Sohi, *Look What I Did with a Leaf!* (1993)

Mary Winston, *American Heart Association Kids' Cookbook* (1993)

Mini-lesson:

"I want to share a really different kind of nonfiction, "how-to" books. These books help us learn how to do things. Many of you probably have one kind of how-to book in your kitchen. Who has a cookbook? Well, that is a how-to book. It teaches us how to cook. But there are many more things this kind of nonfiction teaches us…"

Main nonfiction characteristics:

• formats of recipe directions (list, expository)

• materials/ingredients lists

• illustrated/photographed directions

Thursday

Books:

Simon Bell and Alexandra Parsons, *What's Inside My Body?* (1991)

Rita Golden Gelman, *Body Battles* (1992)

Sandra Markle, *Outside and Inside You* (1991)

Mini-lesson:

"Sometimes nonfiction writers use a story to report a lot of information. They want to give readers information, but they think they can do it better in a story. It's kind of a trick that nonfiction writers use sometimes." (After reading *Body Battles:* "Did Rita Gelman give a lot of information? Did she write this book to tell a story or to teach us about our bodies?")

Main nonfiction characteristic:

using fiction in writing nonfiction

Additional characteristics:

• humor

• credits

• cross-sectioned drawings

• enlarged photographs, X rays, heat sensitive photography

• glossary/index

Friday

Books:

Rosmarie Hausherr, *What Instrument Is This?* (1994)

Karla Kuskin, *The Philharmonic Gets Dressed* (1982)

Scholastic First Discovery Books, *Musical Instruments* (1992)
Barrie Turner, *I Like Music* (1989)

Mini-lesson:

"Sometimes nonfiction writers begin parts of the book with a question so that readers will start to wonder what the answer might be before they read it. The question might also help readers decide they are not interested in this part!"

Main nonfiction characteristic:

lead with a question

Additional characteristics:

• use of story
• organizational differences
• cross-sectioned drawings
• use of photographs vs. drawings
• how-to information

Our comparison of books on the same topic continues for about two weeks. Then, during the last week or two of the nonfiction genre study, I select one book to illustrate some particular characteristic unique to nonfiction. The final week's mini-lessons might introduce new characteristics or reinforce those we have already discussed, or they may incorporate children's experience as we explore the genre with growing familiarity.

One day, as a part of a mini-lesson, the children and I consider the possibility that a reader may not want to read an entire book, that a reader might simply want to find one piece of information or look at the pictures and read the captions. Unlike fiction, nonfiction allows these options. I discuss the table of contents, the glossary, and the index as tools to help readers do just that. For many children this is a liberating lesson. (They will often admit "*I* do that!" with relief.) Since their early literacy experiences have been dominated by fiction, children consider it normal to read from the beginning of a book to the end. Those whose interest level surpasses their reading level welcome this permission to read part of a book to satisfy their curiosity or carry out an investigation.

The Unhuggables (National Wildlife Federation 1988) is a good example of the kind of book I use in this mini-lesson. I read the irresistible main headings in the table of contents (Figure 3.2) and then selections requested by children to model a way for readers to tailor reading to a specific interest. I refer to the table of contents and the index several times

Figure 3.2 *Table of contents used in a nonfiction genre study mini-lesson.*

during the mini-lesson. *The Unhuggables* also has a nicely organized credits page that can be used to introduce the concept of photographic credits.

One year, in response to the chapter title "Blood Lovers," Jeremy commented, "Ticks suck blood. Does that book tell about ticks? My dog gets ticks and my dad has to pull them off with pliers. Then he steps on them and blood squirts out! But he really *has* to step on the ticks because they are dangerous to dogs and to people. That's what my dad said." I proceeded to check *The Unhuggables* for information on ticks. I sensed that Jeremy's story made some children uneasy and hoped that the book would somehow improve the image of the tick. Under the enlarged photographs of ticks, the caption said, "A tick waits for a next meal on a fern (above). When a person or animal brushes by, the tick latches on and digs its head into the skin. As the tick feeds, it swells with blood, as this dog tick has done (right)" (p. 74). When I had finished reading, Al directed a question to Jeremy. "Did blood really squirt out when your dad stepped on it?"

As the children become more familiar with nonfiction, their enthusiasm grows. They begin to look for certain elements, such as glossaries and indexes, and express disappointment when these are missing.

Nonfiction Series Books

Nonfiction series books offer consistency, which is helpful in pointing out conventional book format (for example, index, maps with keys, glossary, pronunciation guide). One series I have used in mini-lessons is the

Friends in Danger series (Greene 1993). Many children in the class have already explored one or more of the books in this series over the course of the year. I read one book aloud from cover to cover on a topic we have discussed in class and then ask the children to help me recall situations in which the format served a specific need. Each volume in the Friends in Danger series includes a table of contents, photograph captions, a "What You Can Do" page, a map locating habitat areas, a "more facts" page, a glossary, and an index. I point out that these same conventions appear in many, but not all, nonfiction books. Individual children then volunteer examples in which they had wondered about or successfully used these conventions and others from other books:

> "When Adam saw the bird with red wings and he wanted to find out its name, the habitat maps in his book helped him find which bird it might be and which birds it could not be, since he saw the bird in New York."

> "When Kala was excited that we would march in our school's Chinese New Year Parade, she found the page that told about the parade by looking in the index in *Chinese New Year*" (MacMillan 1993).

> "When we were reading about the glucose that a tree makes, we looked in the glossary to find out what glucose was and we learned that it is a kind of food for trees, a sugar. We were reading in *Outside and Inside Trees*" (Markle 1993).

This "remembering" exercise, combined with further examples of various formats, helps children become familiar with nonfiction and may inspire experimentation. Learning about format conventions emphasizes their role as useful tools for research. Children encounter them as readers before they begin to use them as writers.

Visual Information

John and Mack were hunched over Stephen Biesty's *Cross-Sections Man-of-War* (1993), which John was ready to return to the library. The book features cutaway drawings (called cross sections) of an eighteenth-century warship. John was telling Mack, "I can't read all of this but I can read some of it. Look, Mrs. Duthie, this guy is bleeding. What happened?"

Before I could respond, Mack pointed to the caption: "Follow this line. It tells you what's happening in that part of the picture. I had this book once. It's so cool!" "Oooh! Look at this! It tells how to do a tattoo!"

When their reading skill and experience allow it, these boys will revisit this book. But even now, their familiarity with nonfiction enables them to wander through it, asking and answering questions. The inviting visual information carries the text.

Visual images are powerful tools for most young children, but for some, they become life-savers. The graphs, maps, diagrams, time lines, and tables in nonfiction texts are unique in many ways. According to Steve Moline (1995) they give power to emerging readers as well as to older students "whose first language is not English. Similarly, students who are judged to be 'poor writers' (when asked to write use only words) are sometimes discovered to be excellent communicators if they are allowed the option of presenting the same information in visual form" (p. 1). All students, including those who are able to gather and display information visually better than in any other way, need to have the opportunity to examine and experiment with visual techniques in a context that values this method of presenting information. Moline's book, *I See What You Mean: Children at Work with Visual Information*, is a rich teacher resource guide to visual presentation.

Young children acquire information from the visual images accompanying environmental print (for example, signs for handicapped parking, men's room, women's room, telephone, "Golden Arches") before they come to school. Primary classrooms can build on this familiarity. Throughout the school year, as children encounter nonfiction books that feature visual information, I give frequent attention to visual representation during instruction. I have found it beneficial to "spotlight" visual images during the nonfiction genre study through mini-lessons. I select familiar books we've read earlier in the year and organize the pictures into categories. Some of Gail Gibbons's books, for example, feature effective cross-sectioned drawings.

Big Books

Every day of the first-grade year, our class reads or rereads a Big Book. Early in the year, to develop reading skills, we generally read fiction with a repetitive, rhymed text. Later, during the nonfiction genre study, I turn to nonfiction Big Books to give children experience with "nonfiction language" and to show them that a visual display is one way of conveying information. The large size of the pictures allows each child to have a clear view. Some Big Book authors and titles I have found effective include David Drew's Big Books, which offer rich examples of graphic presentation. *What Did You Eat Today?* (1992b) demonstrates graphing in several formats to compare the diets of zoo animals and zoo visitors. It draws attention to the need to choose a graph appropriate to the information. In *The Book of Animal Records* (1992a), Drew uses various types of scale diagrams to compare weight, speed, and height. Children return to these Big Books to browse, to discover, and even to rediscover information. I hear them say, as I heard Charles this morning, "I can find that in that Big Book with the animals. It tells about that." He was referring to information he remembered from *The Book of Animal Records*.

I have used Melvin Berger's Big Books, whose topics include, for example, bubbles, ice cream, garbage, animal habitats, and pasta, for an author study. Children soon realize that Berger likes to insert an enlarged picture on the page to draw attention to a specific point. In fact, for many children, these graphic presentations are a characteristic feature of his work. During reading workshop, after we had discussed enlarged and reduced photography, one child pointed to the reduced pictures in the page border of a Big Book and commented, "Look, they re-smalled it and put it in a little box."

"Why did they do that?"

"To help us remember!"

Christine Loomis's Big Book, *In the Diner* (1993), bustles with activity. Its varied visual perspectives call attention to how to use visual perspective to best advantage. "Why do you suppose this drawing looks down on the diner, kind of like looking down from the ceiling? Do all of them look at the diner from above? Why not?"

Meish Goldish's *Paper Party* (1992) is a how-to book in Big Book format. The illustrations present ideas for unusual, creative uses of paper, while the accompanying story text identifies the project. Children like to experiment with the suggested projects and are able to do so supported solely by the illustrations, a powerful demonstration of their effectiveness. "How did you know how to make this?" I ask, to highlight the point for the whole group. *Look What I Did with a Leaf!* (Sohi 1993), although not available as a Big Book, pairs up nicely with *Paper Party* to demonstrate the same point.

Electronic technology has opened a new world of graphic presentation. Computer graphics, such as icons, make computers "user friendly" to adults as well as to young children. Computers can also assist children in creating their own visual presentations.

Nonfiction Genre Characteristics

"Things Nonfiction Writers Use," the list we began during the Gail Gibbons author study weeks before, grows longer. We add to it daily during the nonfiction genre study as we note additional nonfiction characteristics, whether during mini-lessons or at other times throughout the day. Seven-year-old Joline suggested an addition she had noticed. She liked the way Charles Micucci, in *The Life and Times of the Apple* (1992), used four pictures on one page to demonstrate how a bee pollinated an apple blossom. I added "several drawings on one page to show change" to the list during that reading workshop and later, in a mini-lesson, used Charles Micucci's book and Gail Gibbons's *Monarch Butterfly* (1989) to illustrate the technique to the whole class.

Following is a list of typical first-grade items:

drawings	lead with a question
photographs	ABC order
enlarged photographs	cross-sectioned drawings
microscope pictures	tell how to make something
labeled drawings	a little fiction to make it
put information into sets or	interesting
groups	poetry
several drawings on one page	maps
to show change	good leads
table of contents	good titles
glossary	captions in different print
index	highlighting
write about one part at a time	tell about someone's life
say it in an interesting way	

Some of these items could be characteristic of any genre, while others are unique to nonfiction—a mini-lesson in and of itself. Each year, children surprise me with items that have never appeared before, and I sometimes wonder what the list might have looked like fifteen years ago, when the available nonfiction for children was very different. I also wonder what it might look like fifteen years from now.

Call Numbers

During the nonfiction study, the children's nonfiction awareness soon extends outside the classroom to the school library. The library classification of nonfiction is similar enough to our own classroom library that children understand it quickly. I explain that libraries use numbers to organize their nonfiction books in the same way we use boxes. "We keep baseball books in the 'Sports' box, but at the library you will need to know the number assigned to sports books: 796. The library system uses one more thing to help us, a great way of separating the baseball books from the football and basketball books to make finding a book on baseball super easy. They put a dot after the 796 and add numbers just for baseball. So the 'call number' for baseball books is 796.44. The 796 is for sports and the 44 is for baseball." This explanation never fails to get a "Wow!"

I arrange to have the librarian give a "tour" of nonfiction classifications. Usually, before very long, a child is waving a frantic hand to ask which number designates dinosaurs or snakes or some other subject of interest. (Remember Jimmy in Chapter 1 who, on his own initiative, wrote down the call number and took it with him to the library the next week?) In the classroom I post the beginnings of a list by topic of the call numbers children have used in the library that day. They refer to it frequently throughout the year before leaving for the library, or return from the library with further additions (Figure 3.3). The children also keep a personal call number list in their portfolios (see Figure 2.6).

Topics that reappear year after year include:

airplanes	629.133	bats	599.4
baseball	796.357	bees	595.79
basketball	796.32	bicycles	629.2

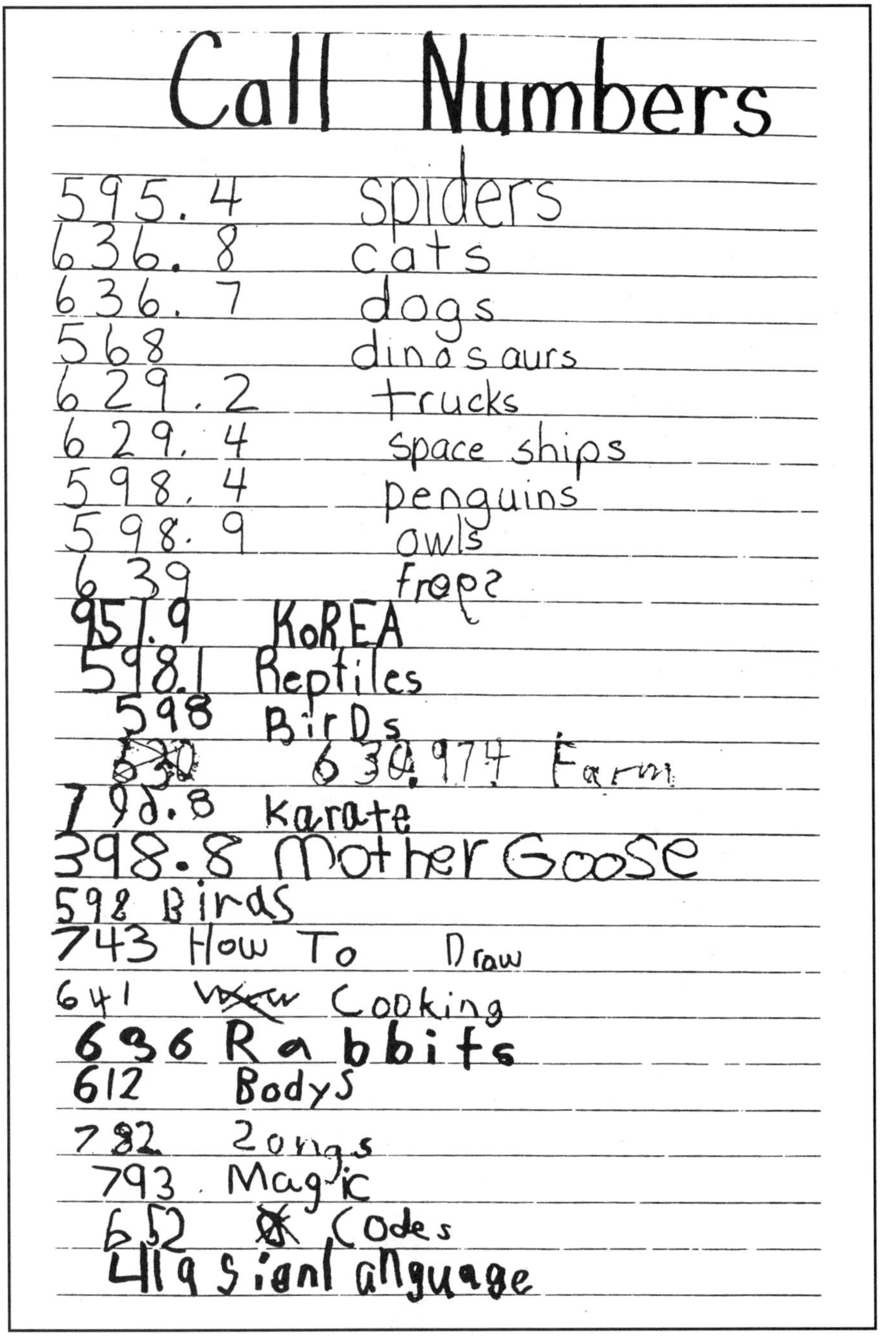

Call Numbers

595.4	spiders
636.8	cats
636.7	dogs
568	dinosaurs
629.2	trucks
629.4	space ships
598.4	penguins
598.9	owls
639	frogs
951.9	KoREA
598.1	Reptiles
598	BirDs
630	630.974 Farm
796.8	Karate
398.8	Mother Goose
598	Birds
743	How To Draw
641	Cooking
636	Rabbits
612	Bodys
782	Zongs
793	Magic
652	Codes
419	sianl anguage

Figure 3.3 *Classroom chart of call numbers.*

birds	598	motorcycles	629.2
boats	797	our bodies	611
butterflies	595.7	rabbits	599.32
cars	629.2	rocks	552
cats	636.8	snakes	597.96
cows	636.2	space	629.45
dinosaurs	567.9	trucks	629.224
football	796.332	volcanoes	551.2
gymnastics	796.4	whales	599.5
how-to	745.5		

In succeeding weeks, as children visit local libraries with their families, they comment on how easy it was to find nonfiction books using their newly acquired library skill. Some of them report with pride that they helped an older sibling or knew a call number that another family member (sometimes an adult) needed. Samantha, who boasts that she'll be an astronaut when she grows up, announced, "I found the space books in the downtown library. It's really true—it had 629.45 on it, the same number as our library!"

Other Changes in Reading Workshop Routine

During the weeks of the nonfiction genre study, children's participation in reading workshop changes in other ways. The most profound change is their willingness to venture into nonfiction as readers, encouraged by new-to-the-classroom books, mini-lessons, and a high level of class energy. Other changes in the children's activities are teacher initiated. Each child, for example, must sample at least one nonfiction book during the reading workshop. In this way, children who are not inclined to choose nonfiction will give it a try. Most of those who initially read nonfiction books with reluctance eventually choose them eagerly. "Kidwatching" (Goodman, Watson, and Burke 1984) is crucial to identify any children not yet engaged. Teacher assistance is often necessary for investigating topics and locating related books.

Sensitivity to children's interests and special needs, and to the need for variety, becomes a central pedagogical issue. Every year, nonfiction proves to be the key to engaging reluctant readers. Giving a "converted" young reader the added support of the nonfiction genre study has positive, long-term implications for that child's literacy. Six-year-old Clarina had difficulty getting started as a reader of nonfiction. Nature did not interest her, nor apparently did most other subjects. In her journal she wrote that she had joined a T-ball team and that her mom's new boyfriend had a motorcycle. After school I went to the library and found *Everyone Wins at Tee Ball* (Grosshandler 1990), *T-Ball Is Our Game* (Gemme 1978), and several motorcycle books. The next morning Clarina helped me put the books on our shelves. Needless to say, she was absorbed in her reading and on succeeding days ventured into other nonfiction topics. The old solution—the right book at the right time—holds for nonfiction as it does for all other genres.

Another teacher-initiated change during the nonfiction genre study requires that the children who routinely share a read-aloud at the end of reading workshop must choose nonfiction. The question and comment period that follows may include further discussion of nonfiction characteristics and the suggestion that we add these items to our list. More often, however, the questions and comments relate to the topic of the book and prompt dynamic discussion.

Michael, a typical six-year-old reader, selected *Castles* (Scholastic First Discovery Books 1990) during reading workshop. Although the text surpassed his reading ability, the topic, colorful illustrations, and transparent overlays captivated him. It took him several days to finish the book, reading and rereading, but eventually he proudly read sections of *Castles* during a daily share session. Michael read the words *dungeon*, *nobles*, *tapestries*, *armor*, *jousting*, and *knights* fluently in context. The group responded, "Where did they keep the horses?" "How do you get into the dungeon?" "I never knew that horses could wear armor." "The tapestries look like a rug at my grandma's house." "I wish the book told more about jousting." Michael sat proudly on the sharer's trunk and answered the questions as the expert-in-residence.

A final teacher-initiated change in our regular reading workshop procedure during the nonfiction genre study involves "Book Talk" (see Chapter 6). A standard part of reading workshop throughout the year, Book Talk briefly gathers four or five children in a heterogeneous group during our daily reading workshop. Children present a commercial for a book so someone else will want to read it. A small sign stands on the table to remind students of the format:

Keep your book closed.
Show the cover as you speak.
Include:
1. Title
2. Author
3. Summary
4. Favorite Part

For the nonfiction genre study, I ask them to bring a nonfiction book of their choice. Questions and comments usually follow each presentation, and because only nonfiction is presented, the discussion more often focuses on information. These group discussion are more probing in their exploration of information and genre. Children's newly acquired comfort level enriches their understanding and enjoyment of nonfiction.

"Look in the table of contents and see if one of the animals in the book is a zebra."

"Or, you could look in the index. Does it have an index?"

"Does it have a map?"

"I wonder how they found that out…that the zebra came back to the same spot."

Technology

In *Young Children: Active Learners in a Technological Age* (Wright and Shade 1994), Daniel Shade encourages teachers experiencing varying degrees of technophobia to learn along with their students: "Do not let yourself be intimidated by the machine; it is just a hunk of plastic, metal, and silicon and can do nothing without commands from you. Relax and enjoy yourself" (p. 186).

During the nonfiction genre study I look for opportunities to incorporate technology. At one point we explored the world of CD-ROM when the technology was brand new to our library. It began when Robby (who does not find phonics useful in deciphering unknown words) read about pikas in an issue of *Your Big Backyard* published by the National Wildlife Federation (1981). Seeing the picture, he miscued the word *hamster* for *pika*. He was highly motivated to read the text because his family had a pet hamster and even compared the sun-dried vegetation diet of the pika to his hamster's food. As he read to me, I expressed interest in the similarity of this wild, hamsterlike creature to his hamster, but I also suggested that we look at its name more closely. Robby blushed and then laughed at his error. "Well, the picture really does look like my hamster!" Since neither of us was familiar with the pika, I proposed that we find out more about it. When I asked our librarian for help, she located *The New Grolier Multimedia Encyclopedia* on CD-ROM (1993). Before we left for the library the next day, I asked Robby to tell us what he knew about pikas and their similarity to his hamster. He even mentioned his reading miscue, commenting that he should have looked at the letters more closely! Later, the class huddled around one of the library computers as the librarian demonstrated how to search for the information. The children were amazed at what she found. We not only saw a color picture of the pika, we heard the sound it makes and viewed a map showing where it lives.

"Do another animal!" the children pleaded. The librarian did a search and demonstrated the range of information available on this CD-ROM. The children were most impressed by the video movement of some animals. Before the brief lesson ended, they were able to recognize what information was available for the animal in question by scanning the illuminated icons (visual images) across the bottom of the screen. Although much of the text was too difficult for first graders, they were able to access information using the icons. Later Robby found *One Day on Pika's Peak* (Hirschi 1986) in the library. He showed it to me and said, "I'm gonna read this!" I share these moments in the classroom to demonstrate the power of technology—its accessibility to young children and its strong connections to nonfiction literacy—and to illustrate one way to encourage and assist its use.

Technology has profound implications for information gathering, both today and in the future. In *The Children's Machine: Rethinking School in the Age of the Computer* (1993), Seymour Papert presents his vision of the computer's potential to restructure education. He challenges the role of reading as the principal way to find information and predicts a change over the next decade to computers that do not require reading skills. His predictions may be significant in how we prepare children to be lifelong learners into the next century.

When teachers consider technology in relation to learning, school budgets, available hardware, and teacher training become defining issues. The teacher is forced to make decisions today whose outcomes will not be apparent until tomorrow. Educators engaged in long-range planning must be aggressive in providing opportunities for children to develop skills for the information age. More important, students must be prepared for the technological landslide ahead and new ways of seeking and exploring information. As Papert wisely states, "The kind of knowledge children most need is the knowledge that will help them get more knowledge" (p. 130). I would add that, in the classroom, teacher attitude is crucial.

One spring afternoon, Libby's mom came squishing down the hall in rubber boots hugging a large jar of murky water. She had promised that she would bring in salamander larvae from a pond near their home, and as soon as she entered the room she announced that the jar contained the larvae. Children's voices chorused "I wanna see!" When she set the jar of cloudy water on the table, however, the children's excitement quickly diminished. They couldn't see anything! Libby's mom promised that by morning the mud would settle. The class wondered aloud if the larvae would be like tadpoles. Then Kyle exclaimed, "The pond field guide!" and darted across the room to retrieve it. Katelyn and Lauren were already headed for the nonfiction shelves to look for a book on salamanders. An announcement that the buses were ready to be boarded blared from an overhead speaker and the children hurried to the door to line up…all except Kyle, who was searching through the pond field guide. When I reminded him that we had to board buses, he handed me the field guide and asked me to hurry and find the salamander entry. "Kyle," I responded, "I will put the field guide right next to the jar so that we will remember to look it up first thing tomorrow" and directed my attention to the class and the waiting buses. Kyle followed me, bouncing like a puppy, to get the field guide back. Libby's mom, who was observing the scene, mused, "Is this how you get them to come back so excited every day?" Contrary to my usual policy, I handed Kyle the pond field guide to take home that night. He returned it the next day with places marked, ready to share.

This story about the salamander larvae illustrates children's confident, resourceful, and excited interaction with nonfiction. The children knew they could find answers to real questions, they had some idea of how to go about it, and they proceeded with enthusiasm. They knew where to begin and felt certain the information was there to be found. But what is most significant to me is that they went ahead independently. All I had to do was to get out of the way!

Each year, before we begin our nonfiction genre study, I find out what students already know about nonfiction and how they feel about it. What is nonfiction? What is it good for? Their replies vary:

"Nonfiction is like an encyclopedia, 'cause you can look up something. My sister looks up stuff in our encyclopedia for homework."
"It's true."
"Nonfiction tells about space, like which planets are hot and which ones are cold."
"*Ranger Rick* and *Your Big Backyard* tell lots of nonfiction."
"It's sort of like science."
"It's like when kids find out a lot more stuff in school, like when dinosaurs died."
"I think that it's when you read about stuff so that you get smarter."
"You can read nonfiction at reading time."
"Nonfiction has green dots on it."

Other comments, in other years, are just as serious in tone and businesslike in attitude. Although children often mention nonfiction as a tool for investigation, they fail to mention it as a form of recreational reading or writing. "Nonfiction is fun too!" I think to myself, but I can't find any mention of fun in children's comments. Yet when we discuss fiction as a genre they are full of excitement, anticipation, and delight. I am determined to add that dimension to nonfiction.

At the end of a school year that had included a nonfiction genre study, I asked the same questions. This time children told me:

"Nonfiction is more funner because you can find out stuff you never knew."
"You don't have to read the whole book, like in fiction."
"You can tell your dad what you found out."
"You can teach people what you know about stuff."
"Sometimes, nonfiction has maps. I like maps."
"I made a map of the pond in my fishing book."
"You can read two books about the same thing and learn more."
"Sometimes you have to figure out which book is telling the truth."
"I wonder if some books lie or if they just make a mistake."
"I like when nonfiction is a story."

"I'm gonna write my next nonfiction like a story."
"Sometimes nonfiction is sad, like *Will We Miss Them?*" (Wright 1992).
"Yeah, but sometimes it's funny, like Miss Frizzle and Arnold!"
"You use a good title and good lead in nonfiction just like fiction because you have to get the reader interested."
"It's easy to find nonfiction 'cause all you have to know is the call number and you can find all the books about what you like."

The time we had devoted to nonfiction had been time well spent. I could see it in the reading and writing workshops and in our discussions in content areas, and I could hear it in children's final comments.

Electronic reference sources will certainly replace the volumes of the encyclopedia in these children's lifetimes; CD-ROMs and other technological advances are already available. But when the shift occurs, will nonfiction books become obsolete? If nonfiction books are used solely as resources for facts, the answer might be yes. But as I have tried to show, there is more to nonfiction, and children are discovering the excitement of finding out how the world works and of learning through their own active participation.

Primary classrooms too often neglect nonfiction, but it deserves attention long before content area teachers in intermediate classrooms begin to require reports supported by three references. Children benefit from knowing how to find their way in nonfiction books and discovering what they have to offer. Shifting traditional pedagogy requires an active effort. Children need a formal introduction to nonfiction as a distinct genre to make it more "user friendly." The responsibility lies with the primary teacher. If primary teachers simply add nonfiction to daily literacy experiences in their classrooms and try out nonfiction genre study, they may enjoy the sight of a smiling child looking up from a nonfiction book to say, "I never knew that."

4

~~~~~~~~~

"You Could Ask a Watermatician!"
Nonfiction Writing Workshop

From the beginning of his first-grade year, Nicholas chose nonfiction during reading workshop. He was captivated by the labeled drawings and charts in the books, far above his reading level, that he borrowed from the school library. In the classroom, he read and reread Joanna Cole's Magic School Bus books. One of his favorites was *The Magic School Bus Lost in the Solar System* (1990). Our reading workshop was frequently interrupted by an excited "Wow!" or "Awesome!": Nicholas had learned another fact. Periodically, he would have to stand up as he read. He couldn't seem to absorb new information sitting down. For Nicholas, reading workshop was an aerobic activity!

In contrast to his animated nonfiction reading, however, Nicholas's writing, usually personal narrative or fiction, was brief and hurried. But early in the year, during an author study of Ron Hirschi, his experience and skill as a nonfiction reader began to influence his writing. In *Who Lives in the Mountains?* (1989), for example, Hirschi wrote, "into a river where otters chase dragonflies" (p. 7). In his journal, Nicholas wrote "Me and Dust are otters and so we are playing with dragonflies" (Figure 4.1). My comment, "You made some fiction from nonfiction!," was intended as a validation of his effort. I hoped to engage his knowledge in a strong area, reading, and nudge him to carry it over into a weaker area, writing.

Much later in the year, during the nonfiction genre study, Nicholas wrote "Here Comes Bigfoot and Other Amazing Machines." In content and complexity this piece far surpassed anything he had previously written.

~~~~~

Figure 4.1 *"Me and Dust are otters and so we are playing with dragonfiles."*

Among other things, he included a table of contents, a labeled cutaway drawing (Figure 4.2), and a glossary:

daredevil: a person who does dangerous things
handlebars: something that you hang on to
rotation: means when something spins
tires: the same as wheels

Figure 4.2 *Nicholas's cutaway drawing from "Here Comes Bigfoot…"*

"Here Comes Bigfoot" was Nicholas's masterpiece. He was proud of it and realized that it demonstrated his growth as a reader and writer. He knew what he liked to read, and now he had produced nonfiction that reflected his reading. "This is my best piece of writing," he announced.

"Why?" I asked.

"'Cause it teaches interesting things. I drew good drawings and I put in a glossary."

"Why did you put in a glossary?"

"'Cause I think people might not know some of the words. I never did a glossary before but I wanted one in this book, so I did it. I like it in my book."

Format

During the nonfiction genre study, our writing workshop follows the format we use throughout the year, which is based on that of our reading workshop (see Chapter 3).

- Five- to ten-minute mini-lesson on
    a writing or illustrating technique.
    a problem a child faced in the previous writing workshop.
    a needed mechanical skill, such as quotation marks, introduced or reviewed.
    a procedural issue, such as editing in another color pencil.
- Questions and comments from the group about the mini-lesson.
- "Status of the Class" (Atwell 1987) where the teacher asks the class how they will use the workshop.
- Twenty- to thirty-minute block in which children write on chosen topics while the teacher conducts large and small group conferences with direct documentation (Johnston 1992, 1993a).
- Whole-group share lead by a child who seeks help from the group.
- Teacher notes, including direct documentation for later reference; a "sticky note" for the child who shared (attached to the draft at the end of the whole-group conference), listing keywords of contributions of children and modeling the keyword note-taking skill; a note to the child who shared to take home to inform family members and celebrate (see Figure 4.3).

It makes sense that the workshops should also complement each other in focus (Hansen 1987). I emphasize the connection between the reading and writing workshop in daily mini-lessons. We examine reading from a writer's perspective and writing from a reader's perspective. When we identify a common characteristic of nonfiction as readers in reading workshop we explore it as writers in writing workshop. This becomes a powerful way to highlight the reading-writing connection.

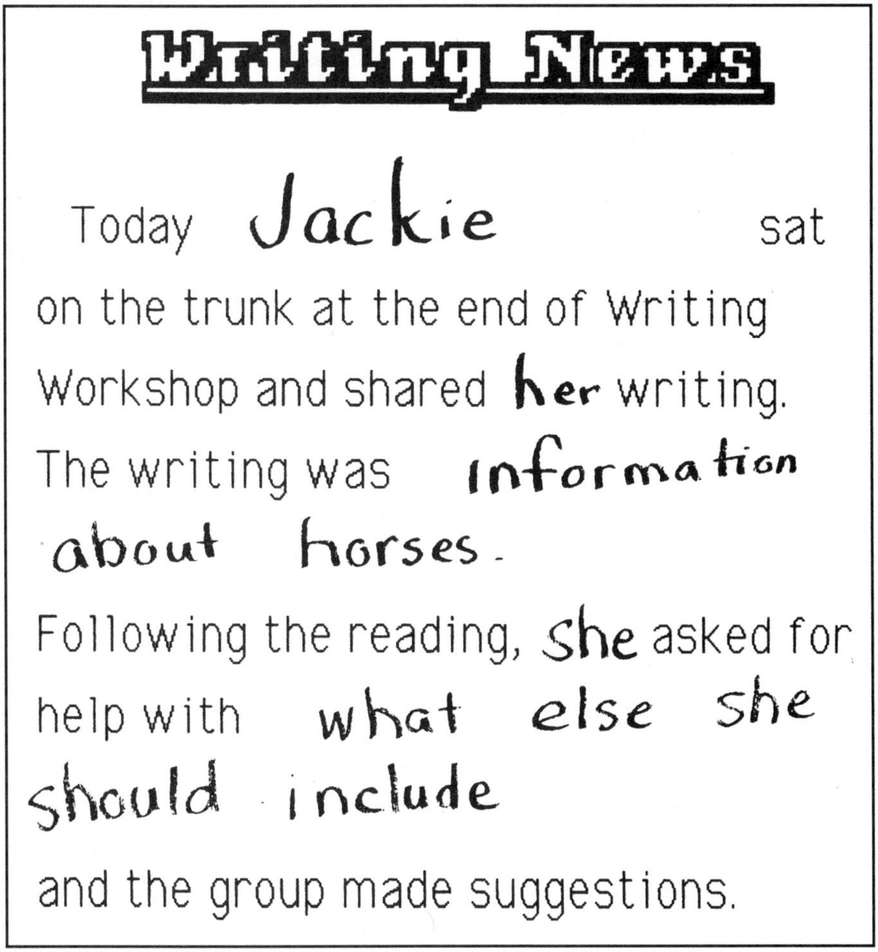

Writing News

Today Jackie sat on the trunk at the end of Writing Workshop and shared her writing. The writing was information about horses. Following the reading, she asked for help with what else she should include and the group made suggestions.

Figure 4.3 *A family note to celebrate Jackie's whole-group writing share.*

Adaptation in the Writing Workshop

During the nonfiction genre study in writing workshop I ask each child to work on a piece of nonfiction writing. As in the reading workshop, this task focuses the attention of the whole group, and I can draw on a common experience in mini-lessons and conferences.

In writing workshop the goal of the nonfiction genre study is to give students the power to express and comment on what they have learned as readers and how it relates to their own life experience. Nonfiction writing "provides students with a mirror to reflect their own thinking about the world" (Avery 1993, p. 108) and "allows the child's voice to emerge from the material" (Graves 1989, p. 81). This goal stands in direct opposition to the strategy of using nonfiction writing solely to get a performance from students.

During the first week (see Chapter 3), I used several books about whales in a reading workshop mini-lesson to illustrate differences in style. The title of all the books I chose was *Whales*. During the mini-lesson, Shawn commented, "They all have boring titles; they are all the same." Later, in a writing workshop mini-lesson, I displayed the books again and reminded the children of Shawn's comment. "Let's have a pretend conference with one of these authors. If he or she asked you for some help with the title, what would you suggest?" We compiled a list of suggestions, and as with most such lists, as it got longer, it got better. Some of their suggestions were *Fat Sea Giants*, *Big and Interesting*, *The Strange Mammal*, *Whales Are Alike and Different*, and *Watch Out for Whales*. I asked, "Could you change a title in your own writing to make it better?" Heads nodded. "Who thinks that they might like to try it today?"

Revision is "physical labor" for young writers, who can struggle for long moments to write a single word, even if their desire to improve their writing is strong. Title revision is a little easier. It accommodates the young child's limitations and unique characteristics as a learner while encouraging an awareness of the revision process. Here are a few ways I "jump-start" young nonfiction writers.

"How-to" Books

Primary-age children are already familiar with written instructions. Most children have watched adults struggling with written directions as they attempt to construct something (shelves, toys, craft projects, and so on) or complete a task (read a map, program a VCR, cook pasta). Written directions are even a familiar part of cartoon plots.

Throughout the year I read many "how-to" books to the children. During nonfiction genre study mini-lessons I introduce one or two in reading workshop and we brainstorm "how-to" topics in writing workshop. The young child, an accomplished learner, has much to offer. One year the children proposed the following list:

How to

build a treehouse	take care of a kitten
ride a bike	skip rocks
make a costume	wash your dog
bake a cake	make paper airplanes
wash a car	make a peanut butter and jelly
set up a tent	sandwich
take care of a puppy	scare your little brother

The logical, "one step at a time" structure of this kind of writing aids children in composing and revising. In the process of writing, children are often forced to address the issue of a missing step. In peer conferences I hear comments like "You skipped a part" or "You didn't tell the part about…"

Mandy Mandy chose to write about "how to make a peanut butter and jelly sandwich." Before she began the actual writing, she prepared her nonfiction draft cover sheet (Figure 4.4). To the question "How will you get the information?" Mandy responded "I made it before." She began with a list: "Ingredients: Bread. Peanut butter. Jelly." Then she move on to the process: "Take 1 or 2 pieces of bread. Then get peanut butter out and jelly out. Put the two pieces of bread together." When she conferred with Jenelle, Mandy giggled at the discovery that she hadn't told what to do with the peanut butter and jelly. She added, "Then spread the peanut butter + jelly on the bread." Jenelle also pointed out that she should say you eat it, but Mandy insisted that it was already covered in her ending: "Yum! Yum! It is good. It's all gone. Now I'm going to play. Bye, bye."

Professional writing, such as Meish Goldish's *Paper Party* (1992), models various ways to give instructions. A child who wrote about how to make blueberry pie did not include an ingredients list but mentioned the ingredients in the text: "I am making blueberry pie today with nineteen blueberries." The child understood the need for specific ingredients but chose a more comfortable format.

Richie The "how-to" mini-lesson prompted Richie to write about his family's purchase of a new car, a kind of buyer's guide entitled "A New Car" (see Figure 4.5). He told me he was going to include a page about "how to" get the money for the car, since that was very important. He wrote: "Cars go fast. You need a car to go places like to the store or to the

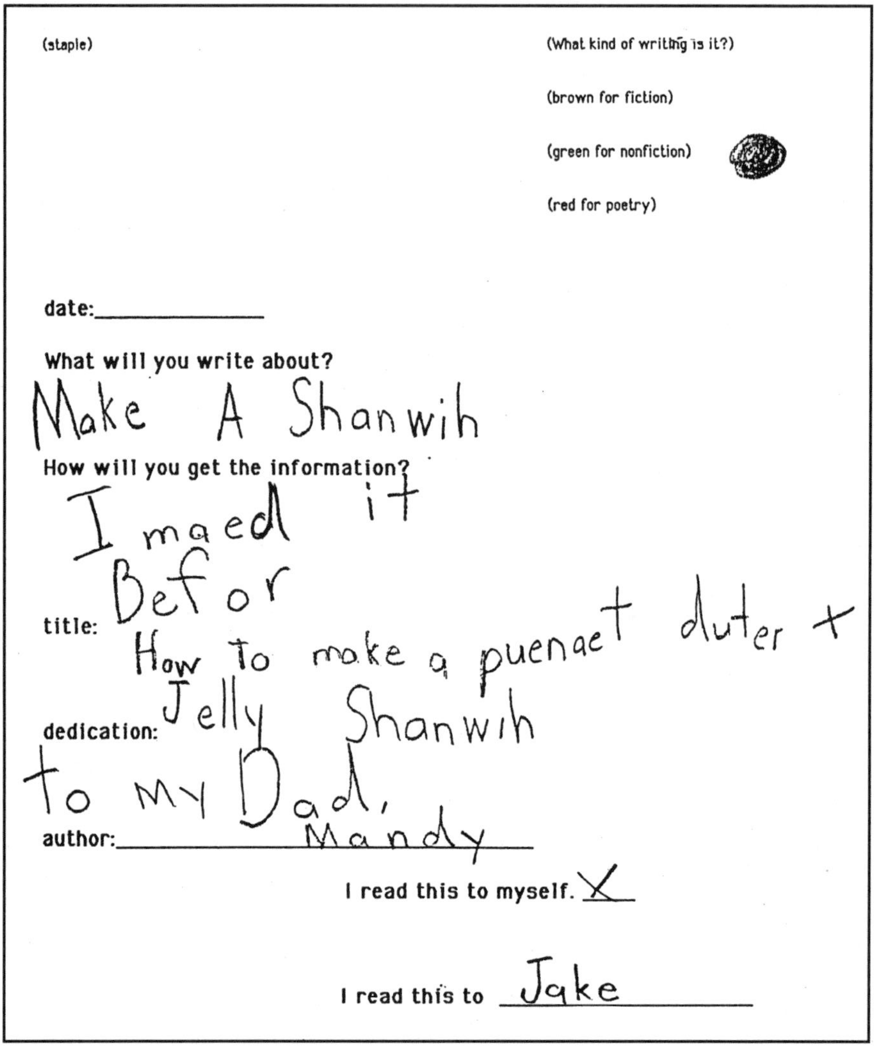

(staple)

(What kind of writing is it?)

(brown for fiction)

(green for nonfiction)

(red for poetry)

date:_____

What will you write about?

Make A Shanwih

How will you get the information?

I maed it
Befor

title: How To make a puenaet duter +

dedication: Jelly Shanwih

to My Dad,

author:_____ Mandy _____

I read this to myself. X

I read this to __Jake_____

Figure 4.4 *Mandy's writing draft cover sheet.*

doctor. Your new car will be nice! People make cars out of metal. What is inside? You need money to buy a car. So you go to the bank. After you get the car, you go home. You have to park the car in the driveway."

Topic Selection

I was surprised by Richie's unique interpretation of the "how-to" mini-lessons. Yet it is this variety of experience that spices up the nonfiction

Figure 4.5 *Richie's description of "what is inside" a new car.*

genre study writing workshop, where we value and explore these diverse experiences as possible writing topics. I once heard Donald Graves say, "Every child is an expert at something." These experts can write about their areas of expertise.

Some children still have difficulty finding a topic, and I offer a mini-lesson to head off this problem. On chart paper I prepare a class list headed "Experts." "Before you can tell other people information in your nonfiction writing," I say, "you have to know about it yourself. So before you begin, you have to be sure you are writing on something you know or something you plan to find out about. Let's make a list of what the experts in our class know. Remember, experts already have a lot of information!"

Experts in Room 7

Jenn	dancing
Terance	camping
Natalie	in-line skating
Peter	bikes
Nick	kittens
Alan	cars
Robin	cars
Kasey	scary movies
Mary	ponds
Marta	beaches
Eric	baseball
Brad	frogs
Paula	jump rope songs
Katie	space
Anna	horses
David J.	skateboards
Sarah	basketball
David S.	policeman
John	recycling cans
Matt	asthma
Karen	babies
Tyler	spiders
Todd	making stuff out of wood

In some cases, children come up with a topic for themselves. In others, another child offers a helpful suggestion. John's father worked at a recycling facility. John had told the class a lot about aluminum recycling, information he had learned in conversations with his dad. When I asked him what we should call his expertise, he shook his head, but another child said, "What about 'recycling cans'?" John's worried expression changed to one of confidence as I entered it on the chart. As the children refer to this list, they realize that they have the same expertise as another child, or they are inspired by someone else's idea. I have compiled a list of class experts for several years and have never had a child we could not designate as an expert at something. In an emergency I suggest "brother," "sister," "school-bus-rider," "Lego builder," "painter," "road-crosser," and other such generic topics. Yes, every child is an expert at something!

Lacey Loose teeth dominate children's lives in the primary grades, especially their own. Lacey wrote: "I lost a tooth. How did I lose my tooth? It was on the end of my toothbrush." She stopped and couldn't seem to go any further. I reviewed a previous mini-lesson on leading with a question (see Chapter 3). Since Lacey had already experimented with the technique to begin her piece, she immediately saw the possibility of using questions throughout. Over the next few days she wrote,

> What should you do if you have a loose tooth? Wiggle it a lot. It will come out. What should you do when it comes out? Spit out the blood. What should you do with the tooth? You should wash it out with water and soap. Put it under you pillow. Then, what happens? The tooth fairy will come and take your tooth and put money instead. Maybe even a dollar!

Lacey had personal experience of her topic; she simply needed guidance in how to present it.

Kenny Kenny was the youngest of five children. Three of his older siblings, who were very close in age, had been married within the last year, and his memories of these weddings were interwoven with instructions on appropriate behavior. He wrote a piece entitled "What to Do If You Go to a Wedding," a six-year-old's version of wedding etiquette.

> When you go to a wedding you have to wear your good clothes and shoes even if they hurt your feet. Don't talk when you are in the church. Don't run outside the church because people are taking pictures. If you see the wedding cake, you can only look at it because you might mess it up. Sometimes you have to dance with big people but sometimes, you don't. You have to go home early with your grandma even if the party isn't even over yet because it might be past your bedtime. Be good because weddings cost a lot of money and you might get married someday too and some kid might lick your cake.

Doing Research

When I was developing the genre study for writing workshop, I took a hard look at how nonfiction writing was taught and viewed in the past. I realized that I had laughed like everyone else at cartoon strips and family-comedy television plots about the child forced to write a dreaded report and the teacher who demanded a perfect performance. But this situation is not a laughing matter for the child overwhelmed by the task, nor does it encourage a positive attitude toward nonfiction.

The report usually involves a long list of requirements, such as an assigned topic, a minimum number of sources, and a specified length. But these prerequisites may doom the project, since they are contrary to all we have learned about successful workshop techniques (Calkins 1986), and quickly deflate children's enthusiasm. Research is usually the first dreaded step on the road to the final report. If we can meet young writers *where they are* as researchers and learners and build on what they already know, it will help us to guide their research and ensure a positive experience. Each year my class compiles a list of the ways they obtain information. Here is a sample:

How did you get your information?
just knew it because I was there
Christopher's grandfather
read it in a book
from my big sister
someone read it to me from a book
saw it at a museum
did it at camp
Melvin Berger (nonfiction author)
made one before
checked it over
watched my cat have her kittens
saw it on TV
my baby-sitter has one
found it near the playground
from the mealworms in our classroom
looked on the shelf in the store
from Suzanne
just asked my mom

already knew it
saw it on a video
went there with my nursery school class
it's on the poster in my bedroom
because once I went to the hospital
asked a grown-up to help me find it in the library
caught a spider and watched it and let it go
asked someone who knew
went in the woods and looked around
used the call number to find the book

When the children and I talk about research, we look at three areas: personal knowledge and experience, interviews, and written sources and other media. Even though young writers may not use all three methods of research systematically, they are aware of them. When I began doing the nonfiction genre study with first graders, I read a book to the whole group during reading workshop. During the writing workshop mini-lesson I asked the children how they thought the author got the information he or she needed to write the book. One year, after I had read *Whales* by Gail Gibbons (1991c), these were some of their responses:

"She probably went to Florida to watch whales."
"She must have gone to the ocean on a big ship and saw a whale real close up, or maybe she went to a circus."
"She probably read about whales in books."
"Maybe she asked a sea captain."
"She could ask a watermatician!"

Clearly, they understood that authors gather information through research and that recalling personal experience, interviewing, and consulting books are methods of research.

To help individual children focus on how to do research for their own writing, I have them use a cover sheet for their nonfiction drafts (similar to Figure 4.4) that includes the question "How will you get the information?" By responding to this question on the draft cover sheet they are aware from the start that sources and research are significant considerations in planning their writing and a key part of the prewriting process, when the writer is deciding how to begin and how to proceed.

Together, we review how we have approached research in our classroom and add to the resource list in writing workshop. I am careful to record the items on the list in the vocabulary of the young contributor. In conferences and mini-lessons, we consider whether different topics require different types of research and conclude that sometimes one type of research is used, sometimes two or three. Children who are unsure about how they will obtain the information they need can refer to the list for ideas.

Personal Knowledge

During writing workshop Cassie wrote:

> The wind blew down the tree in my yard. My treehouse was in the tree. It got smashed. Lots of people cried because the wind made them scared. Some people don't want to go in any treehouses any more. My dad cut up our tree. Some people cried again.

Cassie's piece provides a unique perspective that did not appear in the local newspaper—the wind storm as seen through the eyes of a six-year-old. Her own experience supplied the details to make her point effectively. I used Cassie's piece in a mini-lesson on the significance of personal experience in writing nonfiction. "Cassie had all the information she needed to write about the storm. She wanted to tell what the storm did to a little girl, to her. No one had to tell her about it because she was there, and she knew what happened and how it felt." Cassie had entered "just knew it because I was there" on her cover sheet, and I added it to the classroom list.

In Chapter 2, I mentioned a boy who had found a fallen bird nest lined with hair. He labeled it "Birds recycle too!" when he put it on display because the nest maker had used his red hair, scattered on the ground during his outdoor haircuts. He later wrote a nonfiction piece in which he examined the nest, described it, and speculated about the materials the bird used in its construction. From the nest's size and site, he attempted to identify the builder. Later, in a mini-lesson, we reviewed his experience and his desire to write about it. Then we added "checked it over" from his draft cover sheet to the information source list.

Interviewing

Christopher Early in the school year, everyone quickly became aware of Christopher's relationship with his grandfather and of his grandfather's expertise as a naturalist who explores and respects the environment. When Christopher needed specific information, his thoughts would turn to this reliable source. His contributions on scientific topics were often preceded by

"Me and my grandpa found it and my grandpa said that it…"
"My grandpa told me that…"
"I'll ask my grandpa why…"

Sometimes other members of the class would suggest that Christopher ask his grandfather for information when we had questions about nature. It seemed a simple and logical plan to tap his expert knowledge and have Christopher conduct an interview for us. We added "Christopher's grandfather" to the list of ways we have carried out research.

Certainly, not all children are as fortunate as Christopher in having an interested, available, and loving adult to answer their questions. Yet, most children have had access to adults who have, at least minimally, answered their questions (for example, an older family member, teacher, doctor, store clerk, librarian, police officer, hair stylist, playground supervisor, sanitation worker, lifeguard, bus driver, or repair person). I believe that all children have successfully conducted interviews in pursuit of information. As Donald Graves (1989) tells us, "The interview is one of the cornerstones of information gathering throughout the child's career as a learner" (p. 20). According to Linda Rief (1985), "the process involved in using the gathered material [from primary sources] is invaluable to students as writers" (p. 134).

Young children rely heavily on interviews for information, so classroom validation of this type of research is essential. "Whom could you ask?" I say to the child who requires additional information on a subject. If the child decides on a source, I restate and clarify the purpose of the interview and make a note to revisit the child on interview results the next day.

Kara Like Lacey, Kara was also writing a piece about losing teeth. She had noticed that children in our classroom first lost their lower central primary teeth and then their upper central primary teeth. She wondered if she would lose her teeth in that order and why the process seemed to happen in that particular order. "I think bottom teeth are 'older' than top ones," she proposed, "because you get them first when you are a baby. So, when you are six, you lose them first."

"How can you find out if that is true?" I asked.

"I can ask someone."

"Who will you ask?"

"My aunt! My little baby cousin just got two teeth! He bit me and it hurt!"

I restated her purpose. "Okay. So you will ask your aunt which teeth your baby cousin got first, the top ones or the bottom ones." Other members of the class suggested that Kara could, in addition, ask her mother about her teething and said that some of them would also ask their parents. Rebecca offered, "I know where I can find out without even asking my mom. My mom wrote down the day I got my teeth in my baby book." Rebecca's suggestion, and her subsequent bringing of her baby book to school, gave us an opportunity to discuss another type of research: using recorded information. It also afforded an example of using more than one type of information gathering, which was fuel for yet another mini-lesson.

To the primary-age child, information received in an interview is significant and reliable, since it comes from a living, breathing, caring source. By recognizing that this form of research is valuable, the primary teacher can set the stage for including and valuing the interview as a form of research in lifelong learning. I usually offer a mini-lesson to review effective listening skills (such as posture and eye contact) through role playing.

I hesitate to present young children with a more formal plan for the interview. For them, recognizing that the interview is a form of information gathering, establishing a purpose for the interview, and following up afterward are enough. What they need most is to experience the process over and over again as a preparation for writing. More mature children are ready to begin to formulate ways of recording the information they are gathering—their proposed questions, their follow-up questions, and the interviewee's responses. Formal recording develops naturally as the information becomes more complex and detailed, and it reflects in turn the child's cognitive maturation.

I find it more effective to deal with increasingly sophisticated interview techniques on an individual basis in conferences: "You will ask about a lot of information. It might be hard to remember it all. I know a way to help you remember all that you need to find out. You could…" I tailor my suggestion to fit the particular situation, giving the child enough direction to be successful in preparing and recording the interview.

Information from Written Sources

Children also interact with text as a means of research, a process that occurs naturally as they gain experience as readers and writers.

Todd Six-year-old Todd was especially fascinated by volcanoes. He was eager to write about them and drew several pictures using information he already knew. He was confident and enthusiastic about his topic choice and, in a small-group prewriting conference, talked about volcanoes and showed us his drawings (Figure 4.6). Then Ben told him, "You should put in about Mount Saint Helens." Todd blushed, his expression changing from one of confidence to one of wonder.

"What could he put in about Mount Saint Helens, Ben?" I asked.

Ben replied, "I know that it erupted and blew ashes all over. He could say that."

After the conference, I approached Todd to find out what he might need to follow up on Ben's suggestion. I told Todd that we had a few volcano books in the classroom, and he added, "And I know where the volcano books are in the library." He found what he needed in Seymour Simon's *Volcanoes* (1988), and his final draft included two pages on Mount Saint Helens, which he inserted in the middle of the draft. In the process of locating this information, Todd commented, " It will be easy to find. We can look in the index under *M*." Ironically, the Simon book did not have an index. "Too bad about the index," was Todd's comment, "I had to get help to find out where it told about Mount Saint Helens. If this book had an index, I could have found it all by myself." Here is Todd's final draft:

Volcanoes are mountains with a hole in the top. Volcanoes can erupt quickly. Lava hardens to form rock. Mount Saint Helens is a volcano but it didn't erupt for a long time. Then, in March,

Figure 4.6 *Todd's drawing of an erupting volcano.*

1980, Mount Saint Helens erupted! After a volcano erupts, people plant trees and build houses again.

Todd's research was neither complete nor thorough, yet he found out what he needed to know to satisfy his desire to write about volcanoes. In the process, he grew as a nonfiction writer.

Certainly, not all children are eager to seek information from the library for their nonfiction writing. Many respond negatively to suggestions, whether from the teacher or their classmates. However, witnessing or participating in another child's search, consciously or subconsciously, extends an invitation to the whole group and gives them a way to locate further information next time. As Todd went about finding the information he needed, he was informally observed by the class. The writing workshop allowed the entire group to log the experience as a possible approach in their own research.

Rebecca Rebecca's baby book led us to add "check to see if someone wrote it down" to our list of ways to find information. Her baby book recorded the dates of the emergence of each of her primary teeth, and each child in the class had a record of missing primary teeth in his or her portfolio (Figure 4.7). The information was a powerful verification of Kara's theory about the sequence of tooth emergence and loss, and of the value of recording information. Children mentioned other records our class gathered, such as outdoor temperature, lunch count, attendance, the graph on selecting the color of our new fish (and other graphs), our fish observation journal, as well as individual learning logs and personal journals, as sources of "information you might need for your writing."

Ben On a trip to the park with the afterschool program, Ben found a fossil. The next morning, in the classroom, he tried to identify it. He looked through a field guide, *Fossils: A Guide to Prehistoric Life* (Rhodes, Zim, and Shaffer 1962), read the caption under the picture that looked like his fossil, and identified it as a "trilobite." Although the field guide far exceeded his reading level, it was so well organized and illustrated that he was able to use it successfully, supported by what he already knew and his keen interest.

Ben then cut a narrow strip from a "sticky note," wrote his name on it and stamped it with the date, and attached it to the page of the guide that identified his fossil. These markers remain in place for the entire school year so that other users of the fossil field guide will be reminded of Ben's discovery. I have seen it happen many times.

Kelly Occasionally, a child will choose to write on an event too recent for the available books. Kelly, for example, wanted to write about the Empire

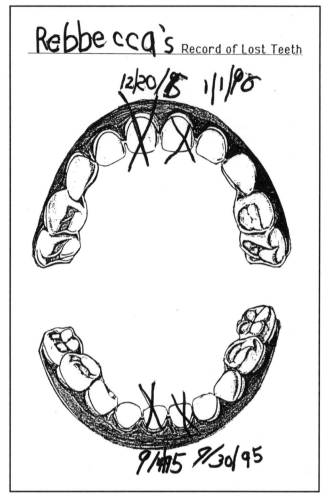

Figure 4.7 *Rebecca's portfolio record of her lost teeth.*

State Games, a statewide athletic competition that had taken place in our community a few months previously. Among other things, she wanted to indicate how many athletes had participated. "How will you find out?" I asked her in an individual conference.

"I'll look in a book."

She went to our nonfiction shelves and found the box of books marked "Sports." Unsuccessful in locating the information there, she asked if she could get help during a whole-group conference. "Somebody probably knows," she assured me. At the end of writing workshop, she asked if anyone knew how many athletes participated in the games. A discussion began after a short silence.

"Just say 'lots of people.'"

"I think maybe ten hundred."

"How do you know that, 'cause I don't think ten hundred is a real number?"

"I guessed 'cause I saw people watching a soccer game."

"Yeah, but Kelly wants to tell about the people who did the games, not the people who watched."

"More people watched than the people who were playing."

"Anyway, it just happened a little while ago, so I don't think anybody wrote a book about it yet."

"Our books were here before the Empire State Games happened, so they can't tell about it."

"Maybe no one wrote down about it."

"I heard about it in TV and I saw all the people who were gonna play wearing blue suits when I saw the fireworks. That's why I said 'lots of people'" [referring to the opening ceremonies].

"Call the guy on TV and ask him."

"Maybe the library has a new book about it, like a book that somebody just wrote."

"I saw about the Empire State Games, but it wasn't in a book."

"Where did you see it?"

"I saw it in the newspaper, 'cause my big brother played soccer and his picture was in the newspaper too!"

"Did it tell about how many players?"

"I don't know, because I only looked at the picture of my brother. My brother knew that somebody took his picture. It was real hot that day!"

"Yeah, and some people had to go to the hospital because they got too hot."

"My cousin was in swimming and it was hot in there too when we were watching, but my cousin didn't get hot 'cause she was in the water!"

As the comments began to wander from Kelly's question, I interjected, "So, Kelly, did you get some ideas about how you can find out what you need to know?"

She nodded. "I got the idea about the newspaper. It told how many people in the newspaper, I think...maybe." Ultimately, she found articles on the Empire State Games in the newspaper at the bottom of her family's recycling bin. Several other children, who had family members participating in the competition, brought in isolated articles.

I made a note to myself to do a mini-lesson on copyright dates and how they can help with problems like Kelly's. Since the concept of time is a developing awareness I knew that many young children would not be able to grasp it. Yet, as is true with most mini-lessons, the seeds are planted. Days later, I heard a baseball card collector in our class say that his favorite player, Cal Ripkin, would not be in the book about baseball heroes because "the book says 1982 and we are in 1995." Another child told me that her book, which says 1995, tells everyone "when I wrote it." Not all seeds germinate, but they did for these two children!

By building on what they already know, children can combine their growing skills as readers with familiar methods of research, such as personal experience and interviewing, to grow as nonfiction writers. The essential impetus comes from the child's interest in a topic, a strong motivation for all writers.

Mini-lesson Topics

In the Middle (Atwell 1987), which introduced me to mini-lessons years ago, also taught me that mini-lesson topics evolve from the needs of the students. The most powerful mini-lessons in my classroom are those tailored to individual needs or initiated by students. When the class is engaged in writing nonfiction, I note obvious areas for mini-lessons. Often, I devise the plan for the next day's mini-lesson during the daily writing workshop. It may address a problem one member of the class is having or discuss an element of nonfiction some children may be ready to use in their writing. A mini-lesson on drawings and photographs in nonfiction, for example, developed from a conference with Anthony.

Anthony In the midst of a sea of papers, Anthony worked on his karate piece. Excited about all the moves he had learned in his afterschool class, he worked feverishly to document his expertise. But when he had completed his first draft, his enthusiasm turned to disappointment. In an individual conference, he admitted, "I don't like my pictures. They don't look like the moves, so I tried to fix them, but they don't look good." I remembered that earlier in the year Anthony had shared some photographs taken at a karate competition. For the next day's mini-lesson, I stood several books on a table, some with photographs and some with drawn illustrations. "Do nonfiction writers always use drawings?" I asked. In the discussion that followed we considered the choices nonfiction writers make about illustration and the criteria for making these decisions.

"Will someone share their thinking and tell us how they decided whether they should use photographs or drawings?"

"I have to use drawings 'cause I don't have no pictures or even a camera."

"You could takes pictures."

"She said she didn't have a camera!"

"Well, we have one at home and maybe she could borrow it."

"I decided to use drawings because I wanted to put in a lot of things and I don't think a picture could get all those things in it."

"I sure can't take pictures of dinosaurs!"

"Why not?"

"Because they are all dead!"

"But you could go to a museum and take pictures. I saw dinosaurs that looked real at a museum when we went to New York."

"I am writing about weddings because I know about them because I was in a wedding because I was a flower girl and I wore a pink dress that touched the floor and white fuzzy flowers in my hair and nobody could even touch my hair and I dropped flower pieces when I walked in the church and I have pictures of everybody in the wedding who was wearing a costume…(deep breath) so, I could use those" (sigh).

Suddenly, Anthony's large brown eyes brightened. "My pictures! I could use my karate pictures from the tournament in Buffalo!" When Anthony substituted photographs from home for his drawings, the photographs brought new details to mind and propelled a revision.

In an editing conference, I told Anthony he needed a way to let his readers know that his parents took the photographs. I found *The Unhuggables* (National Wildlife Federation 1988), which showed him how to do it. On the title page, Anthony credited his parents as the photographers, and we talked about the reason for this credit with the rest of the class.

Later, as Anthony worked on his karate piece, we faced the issue of finding standard spellings for technical terms. Our task was further complicated by six-year-old Anthony's pronunciation and my inadequate background in karate. In a small-group conference we discussed possible sources. As the final copy editor, I was overjoyed when Anthony produced a list from his mother of standard spellings of karate terminology. "My mom had to ask my karate teacher how to spell some of these words because she didn't know all of them." Anthony had learned to seek information from experts.

Micki Micki's interest in flags began with the flag of her native South Korea. She consulted a Big Book, *It's a Big, Big World Atlas* (Rahaniotis and Brierley 1994), which displays the labeled flags of various nations in the striking cover border. Then she wrote a first draft that included a detailed drawing of a flag on each page and a simple text: "This is the flag of…" In conference, Jacob complimented her colored pencil flag drawings and suggested that she put in more information on each page "to make the words more interesting." Micki was disappointed. She thought she was finished, but she knew Jacob was right.

I stepped in, "Let's show the whole class your writing tomorrow and ask for some help." I prepared an overhead of one page of her draft and the next day told the class, "Let's help this writer. She thinks she may need to add more information about flags and countries. She has put one flag on each page and told the name of the country that goes with each flag, just as she did on this page. How could she find more information to add to her writing?" The group's suggestions seemed to motivate Micki, and I concluded the mini-lesson: "Sometimes writers have to go back and find more information. That is an important kind of revision."

Micki's revisions included new information she remembered from someone who spoke about sickness in Zaire at her church and further comments about details of the flags themselves: "This is Rwanda's flag. I think you know why that *R* is on there!" She also added geographic information, which she noted from the maps in the atlas: "This is Jamaica's flag. Jamaica is not far from Florida." The South Korean page included: "This is South Korea's flag. I was born there." Micki had looked at thematic maps in the atlas that indicated major industries and used this information in revising several other pages: "This is Sudan's flag. Crocodiles live there. Beware!" Although the actual text was minimal, Micki tried several types of research in her attempt to gather additional information (personal experience, interviewing, information from maps, labeled drawings). She even drew a conclusion from her research when she suggested a reason for the *R* on Rwanda's flag.

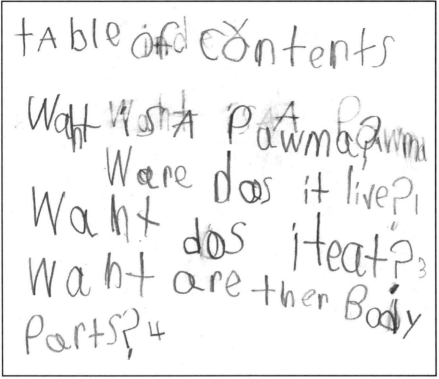

Figure 4.8 *Andrew's revised table of contents.*

Andrew Andrew decided to write about pumas, since he had read about them and seen a TV broadcast that impressed him. He began with a table of contents. It seemed a natural way to begin, since he had seen and used the table of contents in his nonfiction reading. I asked him, "Why did you begin with the table of contents?"

He answered, as if it were simply common sense, "Because the table of contents comes first!" As I observed Andrew's writing process, I realized that he had a valuable lesson to share with the group. His table of contents also served as an outline for his writing (Figure 4.8). It helped him decide what he would include and enabled him to see the sequence of his ideas more clearly. I asked him to describe his thinking about the table of contents in a mini-lesson and illustrated his comments with several books. In the years since I learned this technique from Andrew, I always do a "Some Writers Write the Table of Contents First" mini-lesson. Children who choose to use this technique become more focused and

Figure 4.9 *Matty's cutaway drawing.*

self-directed in their writing. In addition, young writers are more willing to revise the table of contents than the body of the text. Because they can do so at an early, organizational stage, this approach is especially effective in addressing issues of sequencing and focus before the writing begins.

Matty Matty's mom was expecting a baby in the spring, and with excitement and anticipation, Matty often wrote in her journal about her mom's visits to the doctor and her family's preparations for the new sibling. In February, Matty's cat gave birth to kittens. With birth weighing heavily on her mind, Matty wrote about her cat, drawing on information from family experts and her own personal observations. Matty found it effective to use a cutaway drawing in her piece (Figure 4.9). She wrote: "Here is a picture of a cat who is going to have babies. Here is a cat who is pregnant. Lets take a look inside." I had already planned a mini-lesson on cutaway drawings, anticipating the need in another child's writing, and Matty's served as an effective model.

Maria Kittens had also been born at Maria's house, and their birth prompted her to write "How to Take Care of Kittens." During reading workshop, she had been reading dinosaur books that compared the

Figure 4.10 *Maria's comparison drawing.*

dinosaurs' weight and footprint size to those of the elephant, and its height to that of a person. Maria used the comparison technique to demonstrate the size of a kitten's paw (Figure 4.10). "How did you decide to show how big the paw is by putting it next to a human hand?" I asked.

"I saw it in a dinosaur book. It wasn't a cat though. It was a dinosaur, and they showed how big a dinosaur foot looked right next to an elephant foot." Maria's draft and her explanation of how she got the idea became an effective whole-group mini-lesson. I included David Drew's Big Book, *The Book of Animal Records* (1992a), in which he uses comparison visuals. The visual on the back cover, which is simply comparison "shadows" of various labeled creatures from whales to humans, was especially effective for the six- and seven-year-old group.

Maria asked for a small-group conference to help her get ideas for an ending. Near the conclusion of the conference I asked, "Did we help you decide on an ending?"

"I got some ideas but I'm not sure yet."

"Well, maybe our ideas will help you get a new idea of your own. Sometimes that happens."

Ultimately, Maria wrote: "And that, my friend, is how you take care of a kitten!"

Tamara Tamara was writing about growing sunflowers. One section began, "The sunflower will have the…" She crossed those words out and wrote, "The sunflower will wear the seed coat like a hat." I referred to Maria's ending and to Tamara's revision in a mini-lesson on "saying it in an interesting way." Tamara and Maria talked about why they chose those particular words, and I reminded the children that nonfiction writers work to keep their writing interesting, just as poets and fiction writers do. We looked at our fiction and poetry charts, and I asked the children to decide whether any of the things we used in those genres could be carried over to nonfiction. They suggested several: an interesting title, a lead that grabs the reader, descriptive language, sound words, and a good ending. We added these to our "List of Things Nonfiction Writers Use."

Visual Presentation

Occasionally, nonfiction books employ unusual formats, such as transparent, cut-out, half-, fold-out, or even pop-up pages, to create an effect or to present information in a unique way. These features are attractive to young children, and although they present predictable problems in publishing, young writers will attempt to copy them in their own writing.

These "flashy presentations" are one way to address visual presentation with young children. I offer a mini-lesson that displays some of these "flashy" techniques in professionally published books. We discuss the extra planning and work involved and consider whether these techniques present the information more effectively. In another mini-lesson we discuss variations in print size and the placement of illustrations and text on the page. Sometimes children suggest more or less complicated presentations.

To encourage effective visual presentations is another goal of the nonfiction genre study. *Step-by-Step: Making Books* (Stowell 1994) includes some suggestions and directions for zigzag books, pop-up books, page flaps, peepholes, and peepholes with wheels (see pp. 28–35), which young children find helpful.

I have helped innovative children produce pop-up spiders, question pages with holes giving clues to the answers on the following page, a fold-out giant redwood tree, a "scratch and sniff" pine scent (created by rubbing pine needles onto an outlined square on the page), and an attempt at creating overlay pages.

Sam Sam's grandmother gave him a number of shark tooth fossils when she returned from a trip to North Carolina. The next morning he hurried into the classroom, hung up his coat, ordered his lunch, and rushed to get *Sharks* by Gail Gibbons (1992b). When he found the shark teeth drawings (p. 13) he shouted, "Here it is!" and pulled the metal bandage container from his sweatshirt pocket, dumping the contents on the table. We all watched in amazement as he carefully examined the fossils and matched them to *Shark's* drawings. Sam found many teeth from the same type of shark in his collection, and he assembled them to create what he was sure was a quadrant of a shark's jaw. He wanted a copy to use in his writing, so later that day Sam and I went to the copy machine where Sam reassembled the quadrant on the copier. "While we're here," he quipped, "we might as well copy the others so that I can write about which shark they came from." Most intrigued by the quadrant of teeth, Sam drew a shark on the first page of his shark piece that exactly overlaid the photocopy of the teeth on the second page, creating a powerful effect as the reader turns from one page to the other (Figures 4.11 and 4.12). Sam's familiarity with a variety of nonfiction formats, the fossils from his grandmother, the Gibbons book on sharks, and his desire to "tie together" the information drove his research and his project to completion.

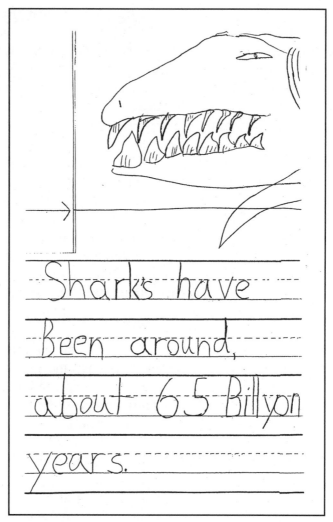

Figure 4.11 *First page of Sam's shark piece.*

"Dumptruck Writing"

After addressing various research possibilities, I encourage the children to consider writing style. In mini-lessons I say, "Let's look at some of the ways these authors chose to tell us about space." In small-group conferences I say, "It is so neat how each of you is finding the best way to report information to your readers. Marcus is using a cutaway drawing. Saundra is putting her information in a story. Joella knows what she wants to tell

Figure 4.12 *Overlay page for Sam's shark piece.*

about, so let's give her some ideas on how she might choose to do that." In individual conferences I ask, "How will you tell your readers about this information?"

Attending to the unique qualities and style of nonfiction during writing workshop can save young writers from producing voiceless "dumptruck writing." My fifteen-year-old son Brett drew a picture of the dumptruck of facts (Figure 4.13) after I told him about a speaker I had heard.

In an address to the New York State Reading Association in 1992, Ralph Fletcher presented the concept of "dumptruck writing." He described it as writing that "dumps" dull, voiceless facts onto the page. As he spoke, I recalled a piece of writing my son had researched and written in fourth grade. Later, I retrieved it from his elementary school treasures. It reads:

> The circulatory system pumps blood through the body. The circulatory system takes food and oxygen to whole body. The heart pumps blood through veins and arteries. Arteries carry blood from the heart to the rest of the body. Veins carry blood back to the heart. Veins and arteries have names like pulmonary artery, brachial artery, jugular vein, and hepatic vein. The heart beats about 100,000 times per day.

Figure 4.13 *Brett's dumptruck of facts.*

The facts are "dumped" on the page to fulfill the assignment, and the writing exhibits neither conviction nor voice. It has some of the elements of an encyclopedia entry but falls short as an engaging piece of writing.

I decided to investigate nonfiction writing in our elementary school. I wanted to compare notes on the issue of "dumptruck" nonfiction writing with Gayla Miller, a fourth-grade teacher who shares my learning philosophy and understands—and effectively meets—children's literacy needs. Gayla addresses nonfiction in her language arts classroom to help save children from the pitfalls of "dumptruck writing." As she told me, "Fourth graders approach nonfiction writing differently than they do fiction writing. It is as if they assume that fiction and nonfiction writing are as different as day and night. They don't see the commonalties, such as voice, leads, closure, and sense of audience. They just want to get the facts on the paper." To counteract this tendency, Gayla invited her students to review the techniques they focused on in writing fiction and poetry and then to list those they considered useful in nonfiction writing. Clearly, her point was that nonfiction writing can employ familiar techniques, strategies, and procedures that are already part of writing workshop and their own personal writing processes.

For a scientific research project, Gayla's class was studying pollination. Some children used the information they researched in writing nonfiction. The children's writing, which combined their personal writing process and style with the facts they were gathering about pollination, was a pleasure to read:

> What would you do if one day you woke up and saw that instead of feet, you had roots to absorb nutrients from the soil, store food, and anchor yourself? Imagine that your body has transformed into a stem to keep the leaves in place and to carry water from the roots and food from the leaves.

This child even included letters from one plant to another to present facts:

> Dear Little Sibling,
>   Guess what? I am officially better than you! I am a Bee Orchid and I can pollinate myself!
>   HA, HA,
>   You Know Who
> P.S. I look like and smell like a female Ecera Bee and when a male Ecera Bee comes, my pollen sticks to his head! SO THERE!!!!

Another child, who found writing difficult, used the technique of leading each section of his text with a question followed by an answer. Guided by his teacher, he was reminded of this organizing framework and was able to proceed: "Did you know a flower has nectar? A bee gets nectar by using the proboscis." While the text lacks the depth, sophistication, and creativity of the first example, it employs a successful nonfiction strategy (leading with a question), which lends the piece focus and gives the child a successful experience in nonfiction writing.

One ten-year-old in that fourth-grade class demonstrated a knowledge of closure, an element on the class list of commonalties in fiction, poetry, and nonfiction, and a clear sense of her own voice. She had divided her writing into sections with headings. The last section was headed "Wind, Bee, Me," and it ended on a note of conviction: "The insect does its part by taking pollen from flower to flower. The wind does its part by carrying pollen from flower to flower. You and I can do our part by not picking flowers or killing insects. It's really simple!"

I read the drafts of children whose writing flows easily and those of children who work hard to produce each sentence. Every piece of writing, to some degree, exhibited style, voice, and a sense of audience. Some children experimented with a technique in the beginning of their piece but were unable to follow through, while others successfully sustained their focus and voice throughout. As teachers, we know that students cannot rise directly from the bottom to the top of the ladder, but we can help them to see and take the next reachable step. Having taught four of the students in Gayla's class as first graders, I can't help but smile as I read their writing, which documents their growth and reminds me of their unique personalities.

Tasha asked Jesse to confer with her on a completed nonfiction draft. As Jesse put down his pencil and turned to his task, he asked, "Is it fiction or nonfiction?" Interested in Jesse's intentions, I later asked him why he had chosen to begin the conference by asking Tasha this question. Jesse explained, "When Tasha told me that it was nonfiction, I knew that it had to be interesting *and* true." Jesse would listen and respond as a nonfiction reader and writer and use his knowledge to help Tasha.

From infancy, children are active researchers who explore their immediate environment with curiosity and enjoyment. Two methods of inquiry, personal experience and interviewing, providing the foundation for the child's discoveries. Later, with advancing skills, children extend their attention beyond their immediate world and learn to gather information from written materials and other media. The role of the teacher is to enable the child to grow while nurturing the child's ability to gather and organize information, in other words, to validate the child as a competent researcher and learner.

As I review the nonfiction my students have written at the end of each year, I am pleased by their attempts to try new techniques. The connection between their reading and writing is clearly evident. I am convinced that reinforcing this connection is a way to open "literacy doors" that might otherwise remain closed.

5

~~~~~~~~~~

"Is She Real Old, Like 30 or 40?"
Biography and Autobiography

One spring morning, with seven books on my lap and twenty-four children anticipating a read-aloud on the rug at my feet, I began a mini-lesson: "Today we are going to read a book that teaches us by giving information about someone's life. It's true. It's called *biography*. Because it's true and because it gives us information, it is nonfiction. We have read biography lots of times before today. Who remembers this book, *In 1492* [Marzollo 1991]? It's a biography. Who remembers this one, *Our President: Bill Clinton* [Bedik 1993]? It's a biography. Who remembers *Happy Birthday, Martin Luther King* [Marzollo 1993]? It's a biography. How about *Stop and Go: Garrett Morgan, Inventor* [Sims 1980]? It's a biography. Who remembers Jeffrey reading *Shaquille O'Neal* [Brenner 1994] last week when he was the reading sharer? Well, it's a biography too. All these books are biographies and all these books are nonfiction. Today we are going to read another nonfiction book. It's a biography about the composer Franz Schubert. Does anyone know anything about Franz Schubert? Well, when we finish reading this biography, you will. Ready?"

An Informal Survey

Although I routinely identify which books we read are biographies, that day my intention was to help children begin to recognize the term "biography" and associate it with interesting, informative books about human experience. While I spoke, I held up each book and surveyed the children's

~~~~~~

reactions to those we had read earlier in the school year. My informal survey indicated that the children remembered the books I held up, but it also indicated that no one in the group had ever heard of Franz Schubert.

Since none of the children knew of Franz Schubert, our reading of *A Little Schubert* (Gofstein 1989) told them all something about him. The book is 153 words long, but when I finished reading it, the children could tell me that Franz Schubert was a poor man who wrote music. They did not remember the name of the unfamiliar country, Austria, where he lived, but Paula did mention that "he lived in a cold place." I asked her how she knew that, and she said, "Well, the book said that he sometimes danced to keep warm."

I played a tape of a few of Schubert's waltzes (12 *Valses nobles* Op. 77) and, perhaps for the first time, the children heard his music. Some listened and smiled, staring at the small, almost square book I had placed on the chalkboard tray, others swayed from side to side, and some even stood up and moved to the strong beat (1, 2, 3…1, 2, 3…1, 2, 3). At one point Samantha commented, "I think I heard this music at ice skating." Samantha inspired me to pass out two paper plates to everyone in the class. Then we "skated" on the tile floor to Schubert's beautiful waltzes. The children enjoyed making his acquaintance.

A Basic Definition of Biography

Since Carla was not in class the day I read *A Little Schubert*, the children gave her a summary of the book the following day. "Since Carla was absent yesterday and did not hear me read the biography of Schubert," I said, "I'm glad you have shared his story with her. Today I will read another biography. Let's tell Carla what she can expect this book to be about, since I have already told you it will be a biography."

The children responded:

"It will be about someone."
"It will be about somebody else."
"It will be about someone's life."
"It will be a nonfiction story."
"It could be about somebody who is dead."
"It could be about somebody who had no money."

"It could be about someone who writes music—maybe rap!"

"We should add it to our nonfiction list" (see Chapter 3, "Things Nonfiction Writers Use").

"We should add that nonfiction writers can tell about someone's life."

"It will tell how someone did something."

I wanted the children to have a basic definition of biography in mind in order to understand how it is like—and unlike—other kinds of nonfiction. I define biography as nonfiction literature that conveys information about a person's life from a particular perspective. In Webster's, the definition is "an account of one's life and character." The children's comments combined elements from both, conveying six- and seven-year-old points of view.

That day I read them Gloria Houston's *My Great-Aunt Arizona* (1992), which introduces her great-aunt, a dedicated teacher, and elicits respect and admiration for her. Afterwards, Patrick said, "That one was just like a regular story."

"Tell us more," I prompted.

"Well, the pictures just don't look like a biography. They look like a make-believe story."

"That's because somebody drew them instead of taking pictures," Lynnie added, waving her finger in small circles.

"That's probably because they didn't have cameras long ago," Patrick told us.

"Too bad she never got to go and see the places," concluded Luke, "but she did get to read about them and tell the kids in her class" (Figure 5.1).

These discussions are typical of our encounters with biography and contrast markedly with those that occurred in my classroom in the past. I would present the standard biographies—of Christopher Columbus, Martin Luther King, Jr., George Washington, and Abraham Lincoln, for example—around the appropriate holiday. I assumed that primary-age children lacked historical perspective and that they had trouble appreciating or enjoying biography, yet I felt obligated to introduce the children to these historical figures. Often, as I read aloud, they would lose interest, but I would forge on, hoping to regain their attention with a related art project after the reading. My efforts to acquaint children with biography were obviously ineffective. Worst of all, I underestimated their capabilities.

Figure 5.1 *Excerpt from* My Great-Aunt Arizona.

Why Biography?

An administrator in a large school district recently told me that in the primary grades the district schools "use biography and autobiography incidentally in the classroom and just explain the genre as we go along. In our schools, we place biography as 'the fourth-grade genre.'" I am convinced, however, that biography is a genre for readers of all ages.

Primary-age children are easily engaged by the life stories of other people—as readers, writers, listeners, and speakers. Let's consider some of the characteristics of five- to nine-year-olds from Chip Wood's *Yardsticks* (1994).

The five-year-old is driven, through spontaneous dramatic play, to reenact the lives of others (mothers, fathers, pilots, waitresses, fire fighters, truckdrivers, and so on).

The six-year-old begins to understand cause and effect and other points of view, and sees rules and conduct more objectively.

The seven-year-old is able to deal with the concept of time and of a larger world.

The impatient eight-year-old explores his or her potential and the broader world.

The nine-year-old struggles with "fairness" to the self and others in the immediate and extended world in an attempt to comprehend ethical behavior.

Many other kinds of behavior confirm the notion that five- to nine-year-olds are ready and willing to explore biography—as well as autobiography. As speakers and listeners they tell and hear life stories with wide-eyed intensity ("Know what happened?" "Last night my mom let us stay up late…and then…and then…"). As readers, they are eager to connect what they read to their own knowledge and experience ("That's like when I…" "That happened to my grandpa…" "Jody's brother did that…"). As writers, they write about their own lives, first through pictures and labeled drawings, and then in personal narratives.

All the indicators are there: young language users are well able to engage with biography and autobiography, which are rich with stories of understanding and compassion, success, and failure. Because biography charts lives encountering the connectedness and disconnectedness of human experience, the genre highlights the issues of inclusion and exclusion.

Young children may lack the perspective to appreciate the significance of certain contemporary and historical events, but carefully selected biographies and respectful, open discussion can meet children where they are with accurate, nonbiased information that encourages a deeper understanding of the experiences of others. I include biography in the nonfiction genre study—and throughout the school year—because it rightfully belongs in children's literacy learning.

Selecting Biographies

Biographers, whether they write for adults or children, are required to portray their subject accurately. Careful selection is a significant issue in children's literature as a whole, but it is vital in evaluating volumes of biography. By definition, biography deals with human experience. When young children participate in this experience as readers and writers, they encounter common human situations and begin to recognize likenesses and differences. They learn to feel empathy toward others. Like all good nonfiction, biography leaves the reader with new information and new questions. High quality biography guides children's cognitive development and suggests answers.

Selecting biographies for primary-age children goes beyond choosing captivating illustrations and lively texts, although these are certainly considerations. The biographies that are most successful with young children are the ones that shift historical issues to the background and focus on human issues. In terms of the reality of primary-age children, who are working hard at understanding and cognitively organizing an ever-expanding world, this simply makes sense. These children are not attempting to put the events of the American Revolution in order. They are reaching out from their own egocentric world. Honest human relations, reactions, and emotions are cornerstones of this transition.

Powerful Changes in Modern Biographies

As nonfiction for children has improved, so has biography for children, and in far-reaching ways. Here, more than in any other genre, a recent copyright date is essential. I have noticed three important changes in current children's biography, all of which dramatically affect today's young children in positive ways: They are more apt to tell about one period or event in a person's life; they are realistic; they present a variety of cultures and minority groups in a positive way.

One Part of a Life

Many recent biographies focus on one particular segment of a life instead of following the subject from birth to death. This narrower time frame makes the narrative easier for young children to understand and holds their interest. Maxine Kumin's *The Microscope* (1984) is such a book. It confines itself to the Dutch scientist Antonie van Leeuwenhoek's research using the microscope. Arnold Lobel's drawings of these microscopic

observations, such as the bacteria in drinking water, are especially engaging and effective. Kumin makes Leeuwenhoek's persistence in the face of
scorn the focus of her brief, rhymed text.

After reading the book aloud, I asked the children, "What did you learn about this scientist?"

"He saw small things really big."

"He saw germs in the water, and I wonder if maybe then they put something in the water to kill the germs, like fluoride maybe."

"Did Leeuwenhoek have help with his work as a scientist?"

Ben answered, "No! People made fun of him and that's not nice!"

"Why?" My question led to a discussion about respect for others.

Realism

In contrast to older biographies for children, such as the d'Aulaires' Caldecott medal-winner *Abraham Lincoln* (1939), contemporary biographies are neither lofty nor whitewashed versions of an individual's life. They are realistic, telling of modern heroes, ordinary people in exceptional circumstances, an approach that appeals to the primary-age child. *Daddy and Me* (Moutoussamy-Ashe 1993), the story of Camera, Arthur Ashe's daughter, written by her mother, tells of a little girl who does everyday things with her dad and takes care of him. "But," Camera says, "sometimes Daddy gets sick because he has AIDS. Do you know what having AIDS means? I do" (p. 6). The story also mentions that her dad takes care of her when she is sick.

After the read-aloud, I asked the children, "Did you know that Arthur Ashe played tennis?"

"Yeah, because he played with his little girl."

"Her daddy did lots of stuff with her."

"He had AIDS and AIDS is real bad because you die when you have it."

"She must really miss him and probably she cried a lot when he died."

"She probably cries still now even. My aunt still cries because my uncle died and he died a long time ago."

When biographies present a subject with sincerity and honesty, children respond on a personal level, learning more important lessons through a realistic approach then they would from a prettied up, one-dimensional portrait.

Multiculturalism

We are fortunate that today, many wonderful children's biographies portray a variety of cultures and minority groups in a positive, accurate way. In her biographies of black inventors, for example, Doris Sims introduces young children to creative black Americans. She presents them as individuals who wanted to help their fellow human beings. *Stop and Go: Garrett Morgan, Inventor* (1980), a biography of Garrett Morgan, the inventor of the stoplight, tells of an accident Morgan witnessed between a car and a horse and buggy. "All day he thought about the accident. That night he had an idea" (p. 11). She avoids issues of ethnicity to focus on Morgan as a concerned community member who recognizes a serious problem and acts with creativity and intelligence.

Learning to Swim in Swaziland: A Child's-Eye View of a Southern African Country (1993), an autobiography by eight-year-old Nila K. Leigh, takes young readers to Swaziland. The text, with many vivid illustrations and photographs, introduces an unfamiliar country through Nila's eyes and personal experience as she moves with her family from the United States to Africa. She is a curious child with a positive attitude, both of which are apparent as she tells about the people, their way of life, and their environment. Her comments are inviting and interesting. I have read this extraordinary book to only one group of children thus far, but their comments echoed Nila Leigh's respect and admiration for the people of Swaziland:

"That girl did cool stuff in Africa."
"She had to learn how to say things in a different language."
"She draws good."

I like to follow Nila's story with *All the King's Animals: The Return of Endangered Wildlife to Swaziland* (Kessler 1995) to add further authenticity. Although the text may be too difficult for younger children, its magnificent photographs bring the animals to life. I usually browse through it, reading captions and discussing the photographs. The book even includes a letter from His Majesty, King Mswati III, Ingwenyana of the Kingdom of Swaziland, and a photograph of the king in tribal dress! Leigh's book tells about Swaziland from a child's perspective as a new resident, while Kessler's book enriches our sense of the natural environment.

Important Lessons

For the young child, biography is often personally instructive. Myra Zarnowski notes (1990): "As they read about a person, children not only learn information, they also develop feelings of sympathy and empathy" (p. 5). In primary classrooms, biography fosters empathy toward diverse groups of people.

Empathy

Empathy is the ability to understand and share the feelings of another person. It is a trait children do not necessarily possess naturally, but one they can develop with guidance. Educators have an important role to play in this process by allowing children to encounter people who are different from them in an environment committed to understanding and equity. Biography encourages children to see that other people also have needs much like theirs and how others perceive, address, and resolve problems. In the often uncivil society of today, children need to experience the positive alternatives to confrontation and aggression made possible by empathic understanding.

Multicultural Education

The pluralistic nature of North American society and the technological advances that are transforming global communications demand a literacy curriculum that acknowledges many cultures. As Peter Johnston (1993b) cautions, we should "take social imagination and critical literacy very seriously" in order to educate "the kind of literate citizens necessary for a multicultural democratic society" (p. 429). He defines social imagination as "the ability to imagine what it is like to be someone else" (p. 428). Biography can serve as a crucial encouragement to "social imagination."

Enid Lee (1994), a Canadian consultant on anti-racist education and organizational change, explains that "Multicultural or anti-racist education is fundamentally a perspective. It's a point of view that cuts across all subject areas, and addresses the histories and experiences of people who have been left out of the curriculum" (p. 19). An accurate and responsible representation of cultures enhances the self-esteem of diverse school populations. As we attempt to enrich children's experience of diversity with literature, we step closer to minimizing the differences between home and school and bring home and community life into the classroom. I introduce primary-age children to biography in the hope that true stories of the lives of others will affect them in positive ways.

A book that sparked engaged discussion in my classroom is *Homeless*, written and illustrated with photographs by Bernard Wolf (1995). The book introduces eight-year-old Mikey and his homeless family and follows Mikey through several months of his life in New York City.

"I wonder how the whole family's clothes could fit in two plastic bags."

"They didn't have much clothes!"

"Mikey said that he usually has cockroaches in his house! Do cockroaches bite?"

"I'm glad that Mickey got what he wanted for Christmas."

"Big kids are mean to me sometimes just like the kids in the book were mean to Mikey."

"If you don't have a house, how does the mailman know where to give you your mail?"

"You probably don't get mail, probably not even birthday cards from your grandma!" [this child had recently celebrated a birthday].

"I saw homeless people on television. Somebody was giving them food."

"Other people should help homeless people."

"Our church helps people who don't have much stuff."

"I don't like bad dreams…like…when Mikey and his sister were having bad dreams."

"Mikey had a cool cast when he broke his arm!"

"One kid in the story said the h-word."

Elizabeth Cady Stanton: A Biography for Young Children (Schlank and Metzger 1991), with black and white illustrations, is a biography of one of the first leaders of the women's rights movement. The text contains the following lines, which produced an audible rumble from both the boys and the girls:

"They were sorry to have another girl."

"'Now you sit down and get out your sewing.'"

"'You should have been a boy.'"

"But when she was old enough to go to college, he wouldn't let her go because she was a girl."

A spirited discussion followed.

"That's not fair! She got forced around!"

"Her father wouldn't let her do what she wanted to do. She was like a slave!"

"I'm glad that was a long time ago!"

"She did have a lot of fun things to do…like play dress-up and ride horses and ride in a sleigh."

"Yeah, *and* she got to visit the jail! How could a kid visit the jail? I don't think they would let you. Is the part about visiting the jail true?"

"I wonder if every family was like that a long time ago or if just her family was mean to girls."

The text of this biography captures the essence of a courageous American's experience and sends a strong message about the thinking of society at the launching of the women's rights movement. It gave the children an opportunity to consider a situation from more than one perspective.

Biography and the Nonfiction Genre Study

Although it is important to include biography when appropriate throughout the school year, I have found that a closer look at biography in the reading and writing workshops helps children to identify its characteristics as a nonfiction genre. Children become familiar with biography as readers and as writers. During the final week of the nonfiction genre study, biography took center stage in workshop mini-lessons.

Finding Connections Between Biography and Other Literature

My objective in reading *The Art Lesson* (de Paola 1989a) aloud was to discuss autobiography. Tomie de Paola had been the focus of an author study (see Chapter 2) earlier in the year. I told the children that I would be reading about someone they knew from a special kind of biography called autobiography. Instead of writing a story about someone else's life, the author writes about his or her own. "So, who would the autobiography be about if you wrote it?" I asked. Faces smiling, fingers pointing to their chests, they responded, "Me!"

This autobiography, I said, would not tell us the person's whole name, but I thought they would probably figure out who it was about. If not, I promised to tell them at the end of the book. As I proceeded through the pages, I saw faces light up as I spoke of the subject's grandparents and of drawing on walls and bedsheets. The last page shows the artist at work in his studio with samples of his artwork—Strega Nona, Big Anthony, Bill and Pete—tacked to the wall. Those drawings helped the children determine that Tomie de Paola had written *The Art Lesson* about himself.

During the discussion that followed, one child remembered "a poem about drawing on the sheets, just like in the story." She was referring to "The Secret Place," which we located in de Paola's poetry anthology (1989b), and read aloud. Other children confessed to doing the same thing—using markers and crayons to draw on their bedsheets! That day, the children encountered one incident, drawing on the bedsheets, two genres, and recalled similar experiences in their own lives. And they were introduced to autobiography. A famous children's author, whom they knew as a writer of fiction, nonfiction, and poetry, had also written an autobiography.

Another year, I included the familiar *Nana Upstairs, Nana Downstairs* (de Paola 1973) and *One Foot Now the Other* (de Paola 1981) and asked, "Do you think these books might be biography or autobiography, or is the library right to put them on the shelves with the fiction books?"

The Art Lesson is the simple story of a boy's life, and that too is part of its appeal to young children. Another book, *Jamie's Turn* (Dewitt 1984), also tells about a boy, but this boy must respond to a family tragedy. Written by Jamie Dewitt when he was eleven years old, the book draws the reader into the experience of an ordinary person coping with a crisis. It is one autobiography that always captivates the children in my class, perhaps because we live in a rural area and the autobiography deals with a farm accident, or perhaps because it is about a real event in a real child's life. Each time I read *Jamie's Turn* to a class, it sets off an animated discussion and inspires children to try their hand at autobiography.

Children have commented:

"Jamie doesn't have a helmet on when he is riding his new motorcycle."
"How old is Jamie now?"
"One time, I saw on the news about a boy who cut off both his arms when he was working on a farm."

"'I have a stepfather.'"

"I think that it was nice when the neighbors helped."

"It was good that Jamie could go to the hospital to visit his stepfather and the little kids in his family couldn't go because Jamie was the one who helped and besides, he was older."

"Little kids can't go and visit people in the hospital. I know 'cause I couldn't go to visit my grandpa when he had a heart attack."

"My uncle tipped over when he was riding his lawnmower and almost got hurt bad but he didn't."

Biography and Writing Workshop

An effective writing workshop mini-lesson after we have read *Jamie's Turn* is one that encourages writers to select a single event and to brainstorm for ideas that might make an interesting biographical (or autobiographical) piece. "Let's think of one thing that has happened to someone that might make an interesting story, like Jamie Dewitt did when he wrote about the farm accident."

"I could write about my uncle when the lawnmower tipped."

"I know about when my cousin won a trophy in baseball."

"My dad helped put out a fire."

"I know that Michael Jordan quit basketball."

"I know that Magic Johnson has AIDS."

"My neighbor was gonna have a baby and she almost had it in the car…my mama told me that. It's true."

Jamie's Turn motivated Ronnie to write about a frightening event in his own life.

The Accident: A True Story
(dedicated to my Daddy and my brother and my Grandma)
When I got home from school, I went down to the water. I was looking for fish. I fell in the water. I turned blue. I was under for three or four minutes. My brother saved my life. My brother got my Daddy. I wasn't safe. My Daddy breathed into my mouth. My Grandma got the ambulance. I had to go to the hospital. My Grandpa got one of my boots. My Uncle Bob's brother found the other one. The doctors got me back alive. They gave me shots.

When I tell my story about falling in the water, my Daddy cries a lot.

The focus of Ronnie's piece and its timing suggested to me that Ronnie had identified with Jamie and felt empathy for him when he learned about the crisis situation Jamie faced.

In writing workshop mini-lessons, I model writing on a biographical subject, talking my way through my thought processes and decisions as I write. Here is an example of one such mini-lesson:

Choose one event to tell something important about a person. ("I want to write about my grandma. She could sew really well and she made beautiful things for people. I wanted to do that too, so she taught me to sew.")

Give information that helps the reader know exactly what the person did. ("I think I'll tell about how she brought me scraps of cloth from her sewing and helped me cut out and sew doll clothes from those scraps.")

Give information about other people or things that will help the reader understand what you want to say about the person. ("I'll tell about how busy she was but that she always found time for me and that when I made mistakes, she would show me how to fix them. I'll tell how she would touch my shoulder as I sewed and softly whisper, 'Small stitches, all the same size, good, good…small stitches, all the same size…good, good.'")

On the first day, I sketch out a draft version and spend the following days revising. I think it is vitally important that children see their teacher struggling with writing, so often I compose as they watch. I work on one section of the text at a time on the overhead projector or on chart paper. We discuss what I might add to make it better, and the next day, I show them the results of the previous day's discussion.

In writing workshop, children usually choose to write about a family member, as I did, or about a sports hero. The following sentences are excerpted from their work:

"I am 6. My mom is 31. Happy 31th Birthday, Mom."
"My grandma lives in Long Island in a red house. My grandma is 60."

"I'm a Mexican. I'm not white. I'm tan."

"My dad almost went in the army but he didn't because he decided he didn't want to fight. He decided to marry Karen. They had three kids and one of the kids is me."

"My grandma likes to read to me and Kevin if Shannon would stay still."

"My dad used to play baseball. He plays baseball with me sometimes. He watches it on TV a lot."

"Michael Jordan used to play basketball but now he plays baseball but he played basketball better."

"My mom goes to school like me."

"My cousin Andrew collects baseball cards and stamps. He gives me piggy-back rides."

"My brother is a pain. He messes up all my stuff."

"My grandma likes to cook chicken" [Figure 5.2].

"My daddy sees me on every holiday sometimes. Next year, my daddy will come to see me on Christmas because next year on Christmas, he will have snow tires. This year, he had no snow tires so I cried."

"My mom comes to my school on Tuesday. I'm glad she does. We have fun days in school."

Children who choose to write biography usually have an additional motivation: they can't wait to show their writing to the person they have written about!

For a mini-lesson that helps children see one person or event from different perspectives, I use biographies on the same subject by two or more authors. For example, I select books that take advantage of young children's fascination with airplane flight. On two successive days, I read first, *Flight: The Journey of Charles Lindbergh* by Robert Burleigh (1991), and then, *Lindbergh* by Chris Demarest (1993). Both are picture books of approximately the same length. The Burleigh text presents the human side of the event and the Demarest text presents a more historical focus. Mike Wimmer's spectacular illustrations in the Burleigh version are usually the first thing children comment on when I ask them to compare the two books. One year, Kendra said, "The pictures in *Flight* look real. In some of them, he looks scared."

In the mini-lesson I focused on how two biographers might view the same person in different ways.

Figure 5.2 *Excerpt from a child's biography of her grandmother.*

"Kendra said that *Flight* showed us how scared Lindbergh was. Did the other book (*Lindbergh*) do that too?" I ask.

"Not really," Kendra answered.

"Why not, do you suppose?"

"Because one author thought it was important and the other author didn't."

"Was it important or not?"

"It's important to some people but not important to other people. So if you think it's important, you can put it in when you write about it, and if you don't think it is important, you don't put it in."

Some children also pointed out that *Flight* recounts only Lindbergh's journey from New York to Paris, while *Lindbergh* includes more about his whole life. Another noted that neither book tells whether or not he is still alive. I wasn't sure, and a parent who happened to be in the classroom at the time wasn't sure either. Terance, who understood that we do research to locate necessary information and may need to consult several sources, moaned, "Oh, no! Now we have to find out from another biography!"

In my classroom, we often make a human graph to compare our preferences. I put both books on the floor, and we sat in a row behind the version we preferred. It clearly made the point that we may not all agree on which book is best and we don't have to agree. "Who's right?" I tease. "We all are!" Sometimes we go down each row of the "graph" and give one reason why we chose as we did.

A third book, *Ruth Law Thrills a Nation* (Brown 1993) (see Figure 5.3), can be used to enlarge on the topic of early flight by introducing the accomplishments of a female aviator who, in 1916, was the first person to fly from Chicago to New York. One year, I asked, "Is Ruth Law like anyone else we have read about?"

"Yeah. She's like Lindbergh because they both flew in planes a long way."

"And it was real scary for both of them because not very many people even ever went in an airplane."

"She didn't have as good a plane as he did."

"Too bad she had to stop at night."

"She stopped in Binghamton. I go to Binghamton every Sunday to see my grandma. I wonder if Ruth Law landed near my grandma's house."

"I think she flew when they didn't have very good planes…like she didn't have lights or even a top over her head for the rain!"

"We could look at the books and see who flew first."

"The books tell when. I remember, but I don't remember the numbers [dates] of when."

Two children located the flight dates and discussed their significance.

Sue Woodard, a second-grade teacher at a nearby school, told me about reading *Flight* in her classroom: "This year I had a boy in my class who shared a passionate interest in *The Spirit of St. Louis* with his father. They had built a model of the plane, and one day the father came in and read *Flight*. His reading conveyed his committed interest in the story, and it was a powerful presentation."

Figure 5.3 *A biography of a pioneer female aviator.*

For another writing workshop mini-lesson, I read *Listen for the Bus: David's Story* (McMahon 1995), which takes readers through a day with David, a blind and deaf student in a mainstream public kindergarten. The text and crisp photographs acquaint the reader with some of his everyday triumphs and failures. My class was familiar with *A Picture Book of Helen Keller* (Adler 1990) and remembered it without prompting from me. "David is like Helen Keller in that other book we read, because neither one of 'em can see."

"Neither one of them could hear either."

"Helen Keller's book is sad but David's book is happy."

"I don't think Helen Keller's book is sad because she didn't die. She grew up."

"I wonder if Helen Keller's eyes could get fixed if she was alive now, because now we have better doctors and better medicine."

"David's eyes didn't get fixed and he is alive now."

"David uses sign language like Helen Keller."

"David and Helen Keller are pretty smart because it is hard to learn things without looking."

"Sometimes, I try to do things without looking; I close my eyes. It's hard...like...I can tie my shoe without looking, but it is easier if I look. And if I look, I can do it faster than if my eyes are closed." (At this point several children untied their shoes and attempted to tie them with their eyes closed.)

"Yeah, and when your eyes are closed and you can't see, you can think better."

"When I try to remember something, I close my eyes. I think that Kevin is right. You think better when you aren't looking."

"My grandma sometimes tells me to close my eyes and think real hard."

"David can do things but he needs people to help him."

"I like how David could feel the ground shaking and then he could tell that the train was coming. Cool!"

"On some of the pictures, David looks afraid. Like this one" [p. 48].

"I think that he misses his mother when he goes to school. When I was in kindergarten, I missed my mother and I cried. I wonder if David ever cried at school."

"David could do lots of the stuff in school but he had to do some of them different...like he had bumpy paper in his cubby so that he could find the cubby by feeling it instead of looking for his name, because he can't see."

"Too bad David didn't have a friend at school the first day because I was glad I had a friend in my class the first day."

Biography "Carry-Overs"

Biography read-alouds become an integral part of our group experience. The messages of these life stories surface and resurface throughout the year as children refer back to them in class conversations. By discovering how people live in different times and places, the children begin to consider situations from more than their own perspective and to judge or criticize the unfamiliar or different less quickly.

Pat On the last day of school, as we were discussing summer plans, new classes, and teachers for the coming fall, Pat announced, "Next year, I'm gonna be a friend to someone who looks scared on the first day of school …like, remember the boy who was blind in that book?"

Lindsey Once a child from our class was injured on the playground. Many children had seen him fall and talked about the event while we waited to find out if his arm, wrist, or hand was broken. One witness reported, "His whole arm bent in half and when the nurse got there, she said it was broken. He cried real hard and they took him inside. He had to go to the hospital." Lindsey suggested that we help this injured child when he returned to school the next day, just as everyone helped Jamie's stepfather (*Jamie's Turn*) after his accident. It was a suggestion that didn't need further discussion.

Keith One year, after we read *Learning to Swim in Swaziland*, Keith wondered if Geert, our high school morning helper who spends the first half-hour of each day with us as a volunteer, thought that America was different or funny when he first came here from Belgium. "You know, like that girl who learned to swim when she went to live in Africa. She found lots of things that were different, and I wonder if Geert does."

Katrina *Homeless* inspired Katrina to write "Homeless People" and dedicate it to Mikey, its author.

> Some people do not have a home. They have to sleep outside sometimes. Sometimes they have to sleep with bugs on them. When it rains, they get wet. We can help them. Ask grown-ups to help them. Would you like it if you didn't have a house?

Hannah The origin of the word bibliotherapy (using books to heal bodily disorders) is Greek. Sawyer and Comer (1991) tell us that bibliotherapy is a useful way to help children understand and cope with difficult situations. Books can offer "information, mutuality, empathy, options for action, and reaffirmation of life" (p. 176). Biography is especially effective, since children read about someone—a real person—who has faced a similar problem.

A few years ago, Hannah, a student in our class, had had a malignancy removed over the summer and was undergoing chemotherapy when school began. I will never forget Hannah and her family's courage and strength. During her ordeal, Hannah needed to be treated like an ordinary member of our group who simply happened to be sick. Some wonderful folks from Strong Memorial Hospital in Rochester, New York, helped the class understand Hannah's situation. They brought a doll with anatomical features so Hannah could show us how her kidney was removed, and explained that chemotherapy was medicine that unfortunately makes you sicker before it makes you better.

The people from Strong Memorial recommended *My Book for Kids with Cansur* (1987), an autobiography written by eight-year-old Jason Gaes. Using invented spelling, Jason describes his illness, his treatment, and his plans for the future—to become a doctor and help kids with cancer. After the reading, our own amazing Hannah confidently shared her experiences and compared them to Jason's. The children asked her questions, and she answered them eagerly. Because we witnessed how Hannah and Jason coped with the same frightful unknowns, we were able to understand that the outward signs of Hannah's treatment were steps toward recovery.

Later, during the nonfiction genre study, Hannah wrote about her hospital experience but included little about fear or discomfort, as one might expect. Hannah's account, dedicated to Linda, a hospital worker, focused instead on the bending hospital bed, overhead TV, and hospital food. It stands as tribute to the people in Hannah's life who helped her recover. (As I write, Hannah, in middle school, is in remission and sporting beautiful new red curls and the same winning smile.)

Gregory We live in a time when children sit passively in front of the TV for too many hours each day. They are exposed to violent and inappropriate programming, which steals large chunks of their childhood. This TV time could be better spent in activities that promote social, physical, and emotional development. Cartoons, situation comedies, and graphic presentations of news all play a part highjacking precious childhood years.

One outcome is that children get an exaggerated impression of current events because they understand only odd pieces of broadcasts and rarely find an adult willing to "translate" events in child-accessible terms. These violent, fragmented bits of information seem to swirl around in children's minds as they attempt to integrate them, often unsuccessfully, into their framework of experience. Through discussion and sometimes biographical readings, I attempt to substitute real-life accounts for the frenzied barrage that children encounter on TV.

When former first lady Jacqueline Kennedy Onassis died, the children were bombarded with TV coverage of her death and retrospectives on the Kennedy presidency and assassination. Little of what the children could recall was cohesive, accurate, or sensible, and their chronology was outrageous! Gregory reported that "This old lady died and she has two really little kids. One of the kids is a really little boy who likes to salute the flag because he wants to be a soldier and ride horses. Her husband got shot right after she died and now the kids have no parents left. It is sad." Another child recalled that "She died. She had on a pink suit and she had blood all over herself. But before she died, she went sailing. She was smiling when she was sailing in the boat."

In our school library I found *Jacqueline Kennedy Onassis* (Martin 1969), a dated work intended for intermediate elementary children. I planned to select sections to read to the class but the children demanded that I read the entire text. I'm not sure how much they actually learned, but they were able to tie some of the information from the book to the snippets on TV and could make some sense of her life.

Sometimes the reverse happens. We read a biography of someone in school first and then children hear and see media coverage of that person. For example, children often come to school with great excitement after Martin Luther King Day bringing newspaper clippings and accounts of television broadcasts, which they connect to the events reported in one of the biographies we have read in class.

The Danish philosopher Soren Kierkegaard has written that we understand life backwards but the reality is we must live it forwards. Biography helps us understand our lives as we live them and live more wisely.

To conclude our class study of biography, I like to ask the children to tell me what they now know about this genre. Many of their responses are identical to what they told Carla when she returned to school after being absent. But they also show growth as readers and writers:

"We learn why somebody did something."
"Biographies help us to know what to do if that same thing ever happens to us like what happened to Jamie."
"Biography tells what a person did when they grew up."

"It tells about someone who was really alive but could be dead now."

"Autobiography tells about yourself like, if I wrote about me, I would write an autobiography."

"Biography tells about a person and I'm writing one about my brother."

"Biography tells about a person but, like, it can't be all about a thing."

"It is real and true and not fake."

"You can write a biography but you have to know a lot about the person you want to write about."

"If you don't know something about someone when you want to write a biography, then you can ask them or look in another biography."

"Sometimes biography is sad because the person in the story has a big problem."

"Yeah, but then you feel happy sometimes because the person solves the problem."

"When I wrote about my grandma, I just wanted everybody to know that she is nice and that she does fun stuff, and I wanted to put in all the things that my grandma does with us."

"Sometimes a biography tells you what it feels like to be, like, blind."

"Sometimes a biography can tell you about when girls weren't allowed to go to school."

"Sometimes a biography tells you about people who live far away from you."

"If they had cameras when the person was alive, then a biography can have real pictures, but if they didn't have cameras, then they can't have any to put in."

"If you write an autobiography, you can't tell about how the person died because it is about you and you are not dead."

Biography enriches the language arts curriculum. It broadens the world of young children as literate and caring human beings. In the words of John Manning (1995), former president of the International Reading Association,

We need to vigorously encourage students to read widely and to read biography and historical fiction particularly, so that they will find in the lives of others some purpose, direction, and fulfillment in their own. Children and youth know so little of the lives of other persons of worth, achievement, and moral leadership that they know so much less about their own. If we are to continue to prosper as a moral people, a just people, a civilized people, and a free people, we need students in our schools whose ethical behaviors and personal values are affected strongly and positively by what they read and what they do as a consequence of what they read.

6

〰〰〰〰〰

"This Is My Best Piece of Writing"
Nonfiction Supports

When Nicholas held up "Here Comes Big Foot and Other Amazing Machines" and told me that "This is my best piece of writing," he expressed satisfaction with his efforts. Many elements contributed to his accomplishment. Some, like his reading, were obvious, some not so obvious.

In this chapter, I would like to touch on a number of classroom practices that contribute in significant ways to young children's nonfiction literacy. These practices buttress not only that "best piece of writing" but also enthusiastic reading, listening, and speaking.

Book Sharing

Sharing books with fellow readers, a practice that teachers of primary students should encourage, can bring lifelong pleasure. Here are some effective ways to support this worthwhile activity in the primary classroom.

Reading Partners

A few months into the school year, Gayla Miller, a fourth-grade teacher, and I pair up our nine- and six-year-old students in reading partnerships. The children look forward to their weekly meeting and bring a book to read with their partner. In selecting a book, they are encouraged to consider their partner's interests, and they frequently choose nonfiction. The benefits of these partnerships are many.

〰〰〰

- Children of different ages discover their common interests.
- Children engage in discussing books.
- Older children help younger children.
- Friendships develop.
- Teachers, as members of the community, also share books and model behavior.

Each week the end of the Reading Partners meeting is met with the collective sigh of fifty children. Occasionally, as we look around the classroom, we comment on the magnificent sight: children helping children through literature.

Literature Bag

While taking a course one summer, I met Alma Kearns, a first-grade teacher from Milford, Connecticut. She shared an idea with me that I have adopted—and adapted—for my classroom, which promotes reading and writing, parent involvement, and genre awareness. In a canvas bag I put two books on the same topic but in different genres. I have used Jan Brett's *Annie and the Wild Animals* (1985) and Joanna Cole's *My New Kitten* (1995) together, but another time one of the books might be a poetry anthology. I also include a response journal and a gallon-size zipper-top plastic bag in which I place a related item. In the front of the response journal, along with a sample response, is a letter to children's families.

> Dear Families,
>
> Room 7 has a traveling Literature Bag for your child to explore and play with at home. It contains a stuffed animal and two books. One is fiction (a story) and the other nonfiction (information). Please read both books to your child.
>
> Before your child goes to bed tonight, encourage him or her to write (or draw) in the response journal—about what he or she liked best, for example, or an interesting fact that he or she has learned. Or, the response might mention something the book reminds your child of or makes him or her wonder about. Encourage your child to write by listening to the sounds in the words (perfect penmanship and spelling are not an issue here). Please have your child practice reading the response in order to be able to read it to the class tomorrow. In addition, your child may

wish to add an object to the bag that is related to the book in some way. (I have added a piece of yarn, and my response explains why: "My cat likes to play with yarn!") The next child to take the bag home will discover these additions and responses. Family members may also respond, if they wish, on the back of the child's response page.

Please send the Literature Bag back to school on the next school day. If your child is reluctant to participate in any part of this project, please do not force the issue. Every child will have several opportunities to explore the bag during the school year.

Thank you for your help!

The Literature Bag continues to circulate among the children until everyone has had a turn. I change the contents, but we keep the set of books and related items on display. This gives children an opportunity to revisit the books and the items in the plastic bag.

A New Library Connection

Sue Woodard, a second-grade teacher, tells a story about a child who brought a book from home to share with the class because he had enjoyed it. Sue encourages activities like this in her classroom: "Later, I sent the boy to the library to show this important book to our librarian and ask if we have it in our school collection. We did not, and the librarian told him she would order it. I always send the child to the librarian with the book, even if I know we already have it in the library, because recommending a book is a direct way to participate in the literate community, an authentic experience. If the book is in the library, the child comes back and tells the class, and inevitably, someone will take it out and read it."

Book Talk

"This book is *Going on a Whale Watch*, by Bruce MacMillan (1992). It's about when these two kids go out in a boat, out in the ocean, I think. They go out and see whales. The whales jump right out of the water. My favorite part of the book is the picture of the blowholes in the top of the whale. The picture is so close that you can look right in the blowholes!"

Book Talk presentations like this one (see Chapter 3) occur during reading workshop. Each child participates in a small group once each week. Initially, I describe Book Talk as a "commercial" for a book you like so that other people will know about it and do the same for you. I tell the children that readers young and old share books they like, and ask them why they think readers like to recommend favorite titles to one another.

Children can bring any book they choose to Book Talk as long as they have read it and would like to recommend it to others. Each presentation contains several elements—title, author, summary, favorite part—that are listed on a small stand-up sign on the Book Talk table as a reminder. When a child completes the presentation, the rest of the group ask questions and offer comments. Book Talk often breaks up with a child asking: "Are you finished with that book? May I have it?" Book Talk builds community and lifelong literacy skills.

I usually participate in each Book Talk group and bring a book to share. But with more mature children, I often place a tape recorder in the center of the group and confer with other children while they carry on. On my way home I listen to the tape in my car and pass on a positive statement or question to each member of the group the next day.

Children bring books of many different genres to Book Talk, but nonfiction is a frequent choice because it is popular with young readers of varied abilities. As Sylvia Vardell and Kathleen Copeland (1992) write: "We are beginning to realize that today's nonfiction attracts even the most reluctant readers. And when students are tuning in to nonfiction, they want to talk about it, just as we do when we are captivated" (p. 76).

"I Recommend…" Bulletin Board

In the classroom we devote a bulletin board to displays on books we have enjoyed and recommend to other readers. On the front of a folded piece of paper, the children draw the cover of the book; inside, they write a comment. These comments range from "It is funny" to "This is the book for you if you like whales" to "Martha is smarter than George." Children consult this display to discover which titles a friend has enjoyed.

Theme Book Baskets

Throughout the year, I "showcase" books on specific curricular themes by heaping them in baskets set on tables around the classroom. A nature walk at school and a hunt for seeds in the food we eat at home could result in a seed collection and an accompanying basket of books about seeds. The basket might contain the nonfiction books *Seeds Grow* (Walker 1992), *Sunflower* (Ford 1995), *Bean and Plant* (Back and Watts 1984), *The Dandelion* (Hogan 1979), *Growing Vegetable Soup* (Ehlert 1987), and *The Reason for a Flower* (Heller 1983). It might also include fiction: *The Tiny Seed* (Carle 1987), *Pumpkin, Pumpkin* (Titherington 1986), *Titch* (Hutchins 1971), and *The Carrot Seed* (Krauss 1945), as well as *Anna's Garden Songs* (Steele 1987), a poetry anthology. When children are choosing a book on a topic, one of their considerations might be genre: "Do I want a story? Do I want information?" The distinguished educator Dorothy Strickland (1995) has noted that "Even in better literature-based programs, the use of nonfiction tends to lag behind that of fiction" (p. 295). One solution to this problem is the theme book basket. Nonfiction often proves more popular than fiction.

There are generally two or three labeled baskets on the tables at any given time. I usually pull books on the topic from the classroom and school libraries, although I encourage the children to add their own selections. Now and then a child proudly announces, "I found this book and it belongs in the basket with the books about seeds!"

The theme book basket collections are a powerful way to tie literature to children's lives. These collections emphasize the point that books give us information on topics of interest. They also show that, even if the topic is the same, the style, presentation, and genre may vary. In addition, by offering a variety of books, the book baskets accommodate children at many different reading levels and encourage reader conversations about common titles of mutual interest.

Visual Representations

"Visual literacy is a life skill."
Steve Moline

Young children are familiar with simple visuals as sources of information in their daily lives. As their nonfiction literacy grows, however, they can benefit from guidance in considering more complex visual representations.

Mini-lessons

Beginning in September, I offer writing workshop mini-lessons on illustration and visual information. The author study (see Chapter 2) is often a logical context, especially if the author is also an illustrator: "Does it make the piece better? Would another way be better? How would you do it?"

Exploring the medium and technique particular artists use (Eric Carle's tissue paper, Ezra Jack Keats's collage, Bruce MacMillan's crisp photography) draws children's attention to the visual aspects of books and validates the significance of visual images. I attempt to provide materials so that children can experiment with illustration in their own writing.

Charts

In my classroom, we keep a lot of charts and record our discoveries. ("Put it on the chart!" is a familiar cry.) I have already mentioned "Things Nonfiction Writers Use" (see Chapter 3), which lists nonfiction techniques we have observed in our reading. We consult the same chart when we write.

The children are emphatic about recording a new item as soon as someone "discovers" it. Our charts document the children's growth (and I jot down, on the chart or in my notes, who discovers each new addition). It also helps me get a peek at the learning process. I watch and listen as children ponder the list looking for the right technique (using several drawings to show change or using a cross-sectioned drawing while discussing change within the text) for their topic, or for a call number before they head for the library.

Parents who visit Room 7 often comment on our charts and ask questions about particular items. Occasionally, I send a copy of the list home so that children have an opportunity to talk about it with them and share the information we have gathered.

Daily Surveys

Each morning when the children arrive, a survey activity is posted on the easel. Since arrival time is hectic as we deal with news from home, bus notes, stuck zippers, and forgotten lunches, the children participate on

Figure 6.1 *A cluster graph from a survey activity.*

their own. In the beginning of the year the surveys usually consist of a simple question for children to answer: "What is your favorite color?" My sample answer appears below: "I like blue." The children add their own: "I like green" (Andy). "Ilkrd" (Josie). As the year progresses, the survey format shifts to more sophisticated representations of information, such as line graphs, cluster graphs (Figure 6.1), and Venn Diagrams (Figure 6.2).

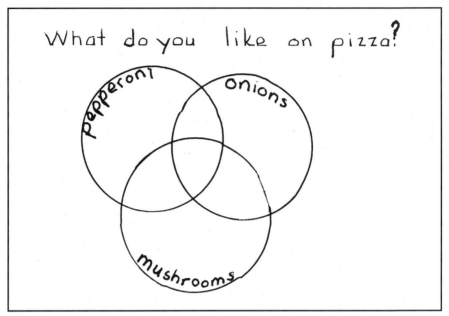

Figure 6.2 *A Venn Diagram from a survey activity.*

As a group we give the surveys minimal attention, but individually the children engage in interesting exchanges as they help each other and observe the cumulative result. They encounter new information and, in the process, learn about each other.

Simplifying Illustration

It is often very difficult for young children to illustrate their writing (even if drawing is the driving force), complete, revise, and edit their draft, and then redo the illustration for publication. Yet graphic information can be powerful, so I devised a one-step way to solve the problem.

I have made up a form on eleven-by-fourteen-inch legal-size paper to address this issue (Figure 6.3). The children use this form in writing their draft and drawing their illustrations The drawing, in the square box (upper right), serves as the original.

Children realize that the arrow indicates where the text will be typed in the final draft and reminds them to plan ahead.

When their writing reaches the publication stage, the typist cuts out the square and types the text onto it directly. This "one-step process" saves

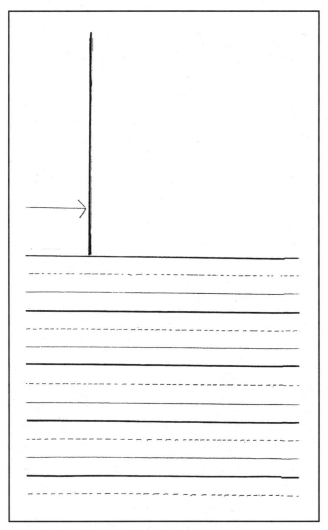

Figure 6.3 *A sample of writing workshop draft paper.*

time and for most (not all!) young children, it improves the quality of the
final copy.

Class Newspaper

Room 7 publishes a class newspaper to send home to parents (Figure 6.4).
Room 7 News gives children experience with the newspaper format,
keeps parents informed of school events and happenings, and showcases

Figure 6.4 *Room 7's class newspaper.*

children's work. We create our weekly newspaper in one of two ways (depending on which seems to work best with a particular class):

- The first uses a school-related journal entry from the personal journals of four children. I reduce each one on the copier and mount

them on a formatted *Room 7 News* sheet. The process requires very
little effort, since it relies on previously written work.

• The second way, and the one I prefer, is directed specifically toward
communicating via newspaper. I ask the children, "What do we
want to tell our families about this week in school?" When the
group has decided, four volunteers write up the news on eleven-by-
five-inch pieces of paper. I reduce each paper on the copier and it
forms a column in the newspaper.

In addition, our entire grade level shares a "First Grade News" area in our
hallway. News to children displayed here supports the notion that nonfiction is often directed to a specific audience.

Parent Helpers

Our school is blessed with wonderful parent volunteers. Each year, we are
fortunate enough to have a few parents who arrange their work schedules
so they can help out in the classroom for an hour or so a week. They help
us in many ways, but three affect nonfiction directly: the parent reader
basket, retelling records, and reading progress tape.

Parent Reader Basket

The parents read to children individually. For some, it is the only time an
adult reads a book of their choice to them, one on one. I encourage the
parent readers to "read the book like a bedtime story," letting the children
dictate the pace and make comments. Children put their selection (with
a name card for identification) in a plastic tub ahead of time. Often, they
have chosen a nonfiction book and talk about the topic with the parent
reader. Giving children this kind of individual attention is a worthwhile
use of parent helpers and a low-key opportunity to encourage nonfiction
literacy.

Retelling Record

The parent helper asks the child to retell the day's reading workshop read-
aloud and records the child's recollections verbatim. This record is filed

in the child's language records and tracks the child's developing ability to listen, recall, compose, and verbalize. In October, when Jackie retold *I Celebrate Nature* (Iverson 1993) to a parent helper, the helper recorded her comments: "These kids were outside playing and they were looking at different stuff." Seven months later, when Jackie retold *Jack's Garden* (Cole 1995), the helper recorded: "It's all about this kid's garden. His name is Jack. He plants a garden and it grows. It has really pretty flowers, and insects and birds live in it. And the person who drew the pictures...I don't know who...drew some pictures that are cross-sectioned. And the book has stuff from the big picture all around the big picture, like flowers with their name...kind of like a label. In one picture a bird is sitting on Jack's head. Do you think that would really happen? I don't but I think the other stuff in the book is true. I planted a garden, but not so much stuff like Jack, just one tomato plant for us so we can eat tomatoes!"

Jackie's retelling records indicate remarkable growth. Each time, she retold a different book to a different parent helper at successive times in the school year. She demonstrated what she knew about nonfiction as a genre, identified several characteristics of nonfiction writing, interacted with the text, engaged in critical thinking, and related the work to her own personal experience.

Reading Progress Tape

Each child has a personal audiotape on which the parent helper records the child reading. The helper introduces the session with the date and the title of the book the child has chosen. As the year progresses, the child's reading improves. The tape documents this growth and allows the child to listen to herself (with pleasure) and evaluate her own progress. I have even observed children's facial expression change from genre to genre, indicating their understanding of how the text should be presented and how fiction differs from nonfiction.

Related Projects

Projects inspired by nonfiction reading allow students to experiment with new information and allow the teacher to assess students' learning.

Projects might include publishing a book, preparing a dramatic performance, or creating a graphic art presentation. I try to help children identify a project as opportunities arise and encourage them to choose from several options. In some projects, my involvement is essential; in others it is unnecessary.

Length of Toad Hops

Christopher led a group in designing an experiment and recording the results because he wondered how far a toad hops during a study of pond life. He placed the toad on a piece of paper, held it gently while he traced around it, let it hop, and then traced around it again. He repeated this several times before returning the toad to the tank (Figure 6.5). The team labeled each page "toad jump" and numbered them all in sequence. One child got a centimeter ruler for reference, and instead of simply measuring the distance between tracings, drew lines one centimeter apart. In this experiment, these children demonstrated the ability to devise a way to record their information, to label it, and to document it using a standard unit of measurement. Although they did not write it down, they concluded, "Every toad jump is not the same." As Christopher affixed the "toad jump" paper to the wall behind the tank, someone asked, "Is that a toad or a frog? I think it's a frog. It jumps like a frog, not a toad." The investigation continued....

Farm Mural Labels

I was involved in another project, a class wall mural, which preceded a field trip to a dairy and sheep farm. Jesse suggested using labels, a technique she had learned from her nonfiction reading. Excited by the idea, the children cut up white paper and identified udders, ear tags, silo, farmer, wool, and so on.

Jesse also learned something about plural nouns. She had written "sheeps," and I took the opportunity to talk with her about nouns that remain the same in the singular and plural forms. Days later, she came upon "deer" used as a plural in her reading. "Hey! This is just like *sheep*. You say *deer* for one deer and *deer* for more!" Afterwards, I documented her understanding of the concepts of labeling and plural nouns. (Not all assessment is quite so easy and obvious, but when it is, it is grand!)

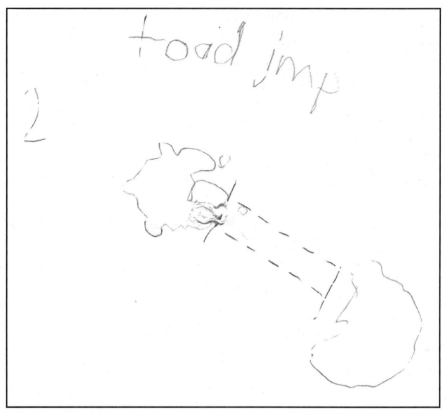

Figure 6.5 *Christopher's recording of the length of toad hops.*

A Book of Planets

I am not sure exactly how Tommy's project began. He was a small, active six-year-old with a bouncy step who always carried some little treasure from home (a spring, a "super ball," a rubber animal) in his pocket and had a legitimate reason for bringing it to school. His pocket treasure sometimes sent him experimenting and exploring, but just as often to distraction. I saw the pocket treasures as Tommy's "security blanket," but I also valued the home-school tie they represented and the investigations they inspired.

One day, Tommy was huddled over something with several other children. Their voices rose steadily in volume. As I approached the huddle, I heard "Let's show her." Tommy's pocket treasure that day was a blue

Figure 6.6 *Research booklet.*

three-by-five-inch spiral notebook. The group had removed four pages, securely fastened them with twelve staples, and were using the resulting booklet to record information. It was entitled "Space Anthology" (Figure 6.6), and its three firmly attached pages contained sketches and basic facts about individual planets. I helped the children focus their research, set a goal, and plan a writing project. Tommy and one other child went ahead with it and each completed a published book.

Habits, Skills, and Attitudes

Social behavior, classroom management and routines, and the degree of community feeling all affect how children perceive and experience non-fiction.

Choice

Jane Hansen (1987) concludes that assigned reading and writing confine the learner "in the straightjacket of rigid assignments" (p. 158). In contrast, in a classroom where individual interests and opinions are valued, young readers and writers have the power of choice, which allows them freedom to grow. By becoming deeply engaged with subjects that interest them, they develop positive attitudes about learning and a sense of commitment.

Remember Jimmy? Being allowed to choose his own path to literacy empowered him. If Jimmy had been required to read and write on teacher-selected topics, I am convinced he would have resisted. Instead, he pursued his interest in farming to grow as a reader and writer, which further broadened his thinking. In terms of his literacy, Jimmy did his best work and made his most thoughtful comments about his family's dairy farm, but it is also true that he explored other topics as a result of this passionate interest.

Most children develop better when they are allowed broad choices. In almost every case I have observed, letting children determine what they want to read and write about produces significant benefits.

- The learner is easily engaged by background information.
- The home-school connection is reinforced when the child selects an area that involves parents, materials, and experiences from home.
- The learner assumes that role of "expert on the topic" and the other children solicit help with skills, which improves self-esteem.
- Choice validation is empowering.

Risk Taking

An environment where risk taking is safe is essential for learning. When children know that their opinions and their points of view are valued and appreciated, they dare to reach a little farther, confident that their teacher and their classmates will support their efforts. When a child asks a whole group writing conference for help with what should come next in her writing, when a reader asks a peer for help decoding a word, when a child shares a fear of thunder at circle time, I am encouraged by these signs of a classroom safe for risk taking.

Scientific Thinking

Scientific "fact" is one conclusion based on the best information available at the time. Even so, scientists do not always agree. When Peter brought a turtle to school, he tried to convince us that the turtle could remain in our tank for a few days. His claim violated our "policy" of returning living things to their natural environment as soon as we had finished observing them. The class discussed the issue and decided to return to it at the end of the day. Later, one first grader wrote in his journal: "That turtle needs his habitat and his family" (Figure 6.7). When the group reconsidered Peter's claim, they bolstered their final decision with their research. Peter returned the turtle to the pond. The next day, he reported, "I think the turtle agreed with our decision because he swam away and was happy to be back in the pond."

"Let's talk about it." "Let's find out." "Let's decide." These sentences are the foundation of nonfiction literacy. Knowing that we can locate information and make informed decisions, that we can work through and resolve problems that arise from conflicting points of view, gives a predictable structure to group interaction. In pondering a question as a group, children:

- rely on their prior experience, consult others, use books and other available resources.
- value factual information as verification, in consultation with others.
- value the experiences of others.
- consider all the information before forming and presenting an opinion.
- value and respect the opinions of others.
- work to reach consensus.

Integrating these skills across the disciplines is more effective than devising exercises. The process of arriving at consensus filters into all the day's activities, whether these involve the whole group or only two people.

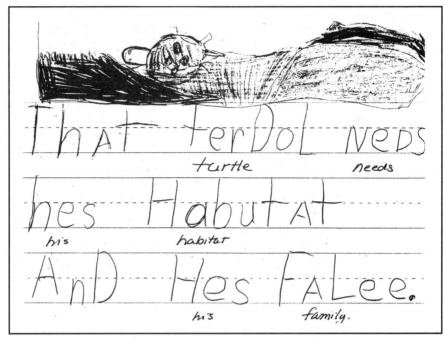

Figure 6.7 *One first grader's scientific observation.*

In his personal journal Casey noted, "I found a toad" (Figure 6.8). I responded: "Where did you find a toad?" (While expressing interest in Casey's discovery, I modeled conventional spelling, sentence structure, and punctuation. I asked him to think about the toad some more to see if he could remember more details.)

Casey responded, "Near my house."

"I wonder why toads would want to be near your house."

"I dunno," and he closed his journal.

Casey's journal entry did not lead to a research project or a group discussion. He responded to my question and seemed satisfied to leave it there. But when Stephen finished reading Byron Barton's *Bones, Bones, Dinosaur Bones* (1990), he said, "I still wonder if the dinosaurs are put together right or if scientists have them mixed up." His comment energized a small group discussion and further investigation.

"All-Genre Mini-lessons"

Nonfiction forms part of many mini-lessons throughout the year.

Figure 6.8 *A page from Casey's personal journal.*

Writing Storage Folder

Children's published drafts as well as their abandoned pieces are stored in a writing storage folder accessible to the child. Toward the end of the year, I pass out these folders before writing workshop and give a mini-lesson on reviewing and possibly revising an old draft. I wanted the children to have the experience of revising a piece of their own writing using what they had learned. One year, Carrie chose one entitled, "Horses." Her initial draft read:

Horses are pretty. Horses run fast. You can ride horses.

Her revision was entitled "Giddy Up." It read:

> Horses are pretty. They can be many different colors like brown, black, gray or white. Horses run fast. Some horses run as fast as a car. When a horse gets pregnant she has a baby called a foal. You can ride horses but first you have to get it ready. Put on a bridle, a blanket, and a saddle over the blanket. Then say, "Giddy up!"

Carrie also revised her illustrations, including a car that appeared to be riding next to a galloping horse, and added labels. Later in the week, I asked Carrie to share her revision with the class, and the children commented on the improved version. "What makes it better?"

Children love to look through their storage folders. As they review and evaluate its contents, they can trace their own growth with pride.

Journals

The morning after the San Francisco earthquake, Sarah wrote: "There was an earthquake. Crack!" (Figure 6.9). Sarah lived on the east coast and had not experienced the earthquake personally. She learned about it from family conversations and TV.

Journal entries can be referred to during reading and writing workshops to help children discover interesting nonfiction topics. I often use them in nonfiction mini-lessons. "Ben, when you wrote this, how did you know the fossil was a trilobite? How did you find out?" "Sarah, tell us why you drew this illustration? Did you think it would help your readers understand better?"

Class Autobiography

Many children write about themselves. Their individual work is supported and enriched by a class autobiography project. Here are three effective ways to develop a class autobiography.

Number Line

We add each day to our count of the days in the school year on an adding machine tape that eventually stretches across the room (*Mathematics Their*

Figure 6.9 *Sarah's journal description of an earthquake.*

Way, Garland 1988). On special occasions (a birthday, a field trip, a special visitor, an assembly), we add a three-inch square of colored paper to call attention to the special day. In doing so, we create a time line of the school year.

Calendar

We also have a calendar bulletin board with seven-inch squares numbered consecutively for each day in the month. Children contribute "something special," and I write it down on the square for the day and introduce or reinforce a convention of print or phonetic skill that relates to the child's news. The child adds an illustration. At the end of the month, I gather the squares, staple them to a cardboard square, top the whole with a wallpaper cover, and record the month and year. These calendar books become part of our classroom library and are frequently chosen for nonfiction reading. At the end of the school year, I have all ten months bound together at a bindery and donate the volume to the library. The librarian shelves the collection with biography and tells me that there is often a waiting list.

Recalling Memories

Sue Woodard and her second-grade class have developed an end-of-year ritual. "At the end of the school year last June, we sat in a circle to share stories about the first day and review the year. I had saved various artifacts—a big valentine the kids had made for me, a brochure from our museum trip, group sign-ups from major projects. We decided to do a brief presentation of these memories for the parents. Each child picked a memory to write about. We invited parents, and children read their pieces. It was powerful. It was a history of our school year, a kind of class autobiography. It helped the children see how history is made and recorded, and it gave the school year a sense of closure. The event was empowering for children and enjoyed by the parents. I'll do it again."

We did a similar activity in our first grade. I produced a large basket of photographs and artifacts from our year together. Each child chose one item or more, wrote about it, mounted the item on colored paper with its description, and hung the finished piece in the hall. The display drew attention. One observer described it as a "yearbook mural."

Some Classroom Staples

Some staples of nonfiction literacy are not so obvious. I'd like to point out a few of them.

Newspapers

Periodicals are very important in my own literacy. For most adults, they provide a daily serving of nonfiction, and for many, the only one. Weekly school newspapers differ greatly from daily local newspapers in overall appearance, but they do report on current events in a format accessible to primary-age children and are relatively inexpensive. They include maps, directions, photographs (close-ups, enlargements, and so on), captions, pronunciation guides, and other nonfiction features. Our weekly newspaper provides nonfiction reading and inspires discussions of current events. Sometimes an article will set off further investigations. I also value the fact that each child takes the weekly newspaper home to share with family members. I encourage children to store the newspapers together and use them as reference sources. For many children, this is the only nonfiction reading available to them at home.

Our class subscribes to *Scholastic News*, a weekly first-grade newspaper that devoted an issue to the 1995 earthquake in Kobe, Japan (Figure 6.10). The issue also included an article called "Make a Quake" (Figure 6.11), which gave directions for a demonstrating how an earthquake happens. We followed the directions using blocks piled on two books. Referring to Seymour Simon's *Earthquakes* (1991), one child said, "I know a book with lots of pictures of earthquakes and it even tells what to do if you are in an earthquake." She showed Simon's photographs to the group and read the last page, where the author does tell what to do. Simon also used blocks to represent the earthquake, and of course, the children noticed the similarity to *Scholastic News*.

Magazines

There are many nonfiction magazines (*Cricket: The Magazine for Children* [Carus Corp.], *National Geographic World* [National Geographic Society], *Superscience* [Scholastic], for example) geared to primary-age children. Classroom subscriptions are one way to acquire them, but back issues also turn up at garage sales and are often donated to the classroom library by older children. I store issues in cardboard magazine holders according to title. Since children often want to find an article or a photograph they remember seeing, or feel comfortable with the reading level or subject matter of a certain magazine, this system helps them find the titles they are looking for. Each year, it seems that at least one child makes major growth as a reader by reading nonfiction magazines, especially *Your Big Backyard*, published by the National Wildlife Federation. Its engaging photographs and simple text appeal to young children interested in the natural world.

Figure 6.10 Scholastic News, *a weekly first-grade newspaper.*

Math Books

Math books? No, not workbooks but books on mathematical concepts. A collection of these nonfiction books, housed together in our classroom library, are useful in nonfiction reading and math lessons. Bruce MacMillan, for example, has written (and illustrated with his own photographs) several wonderful books for primary children, including *Counting Wildflowers* (1986) and *Eating Fractions* (1991). *Monster Math* (Maccarone 1995), *The Greedy Triangle* (Burns 1994), *My Mom and Dad*

Figure 6.11 *"Make a Quake" from* Scholastic News.

Make Me Laugh (Sharratt 1994), *One Hundred Hungry Ants* (Pinczes 1993), and *Stay in Line* (Slater 1996) also offer obvious possibilities for mathematics workshop investigations. Books on mathematical concepts—number sense, classification, comparison, measurement, weight, time, money, fractions, large numbers, patterns, and shapes—lend themselves to many activities, and children also enjoy browsing at random.

General nonfiction books also employ mathematics to communicate information. In *Read Any Good Math Lately? Children's Books for Mathematical Learning, K–6* (1992), Whitin and Wilde celebrate mathematics as "a natural communication system that we can use to describe our world and communicate our experiences" (p. 6). Being able to "read" and understand visual representations of ideas in graphs and charts is integral to nonfiction literacy.

Field Guides and Other Reference Books

In Room 7, the field guides are shelved together as a set of reference books rather than by topic with the other nonfiction books. The children soon realize that these books are best kept together, because it is faster and easier to go directly to the field guide section than to figure out how the required volume is classified.

Anna's Caterpillar Anna attempted to identify a caterpillar in an insect field guide because she wanted to write about her caterpillar observations. I asked, "Will you mention what kind of caterpillar it is?"

"I don't know its name," she replied, "but I could look in a field guide." Unsuccessfully, she scanned the insect guide. Then she smiled and switched to the butterfly/moth field guide. Her previous experience with mealworms and monarch butterflies helped her realize that she was looking at a larva stage. Because the guides are kept together as a matter of classroom policy, her search ended successfully. Activities of this kind introduce children to reference books as a special kind of nonfiction that helps you find facts.

As I sit here in August, planning nonfiction literacy activities for the coming school year, I wonder if the student teacher I expect next quarter will welcome my flexible approach. Student teachers usually want concrete suggestions and activities to file in a neat chronological folder of "things that work." If that is her objective, she will be disappointed. I'll feel successful if I can convey the message that each child, each class, each school community is unique. As a teacher, my job is to draw on everything I know and have done to promote learning.

Certainly, I will share with her some of the approaches and activities that have proven successful in the past, and will probably try some of them again, adapting them to the needs of this year's first graders. Surely we will also invent new ones. I don't know exactly what challenges to expect, but I do know that the most successful experiences we provide for our students will be the ones that encourage them to demonstrate what they already know and inspire them with the urgent curiosity of lifelong learners. If she still wants a statement for her student teacher folder, I will tell her this: Nonfiction literacy in the primary classroom is a process, an ongoing journey to the wider world. If we can map out some of the "ah-ha" moments of insight that lead to wisdom, we will have prepared children well to continue on their way.

7

~~~~~~~~~~~

"This Book Is Delicious!"
An Annotated Bibliography

In the best of all worlds, professionals who work with children would have neither been, nor have I met, anyone in that situation. In reality, we use the available resources. Children can still learn to investigate and wonder, to value information and question it, and to read for pleasure.

Over the past few years, I have been asked to suggest books for newsletters to parents, PTO meetings, a child's birthday gift to the school library (instead of cupcakes for the class), holiday gift ideas, and memorial donations to libraries. The books mentioned in this chapter are recommendations. This annotated bibliography is my "wish list" and a celebration of children's nonfiction books. I have reviewed all the titles here and the search was truly a pleasure. I often imagined a particular book in the lap of a particular child. Once, when I had the opportunity to match "child and perfect book," the child told me, "This book is delicious!"

Archambault, John. 1996. *The Birth of a Whale*. Illus. Janet Skiles. Parsippany, NJ: Silver Press. 48pp.
TOPIC: **humpback whale**
TEACHING FEATURES: **use of story; supplemental information**
With respect and awe, the author takes us to the underwater world of the humpback whale as it communicates with its partner. The reader observes a birthing and anxiously anticipates the calf's first breath of air when it surfaces. The pages come alive with the beauty and grace of the humpback whale.
Arnosky, Jim. 1993. *Crinkleroot's 25 Fish Every Child Should Know*. New York: Bradbury Press. 26pp.
TOPIC: **fish**

~~~~

TEACHING FEATURES: **labeling; friendly letter**

The book begins with a two-page letter from Crinkleroot, "a friend to all animals." On the remaining pages are labeled illustrations of twelve freshwater fish and thirteen saltwater fish. The simple drawings beg identification, comparison, and further investigation. The author has written a similar book on birds.

Asch, Frank. 1995. *Water*. New York: Harcourt Brace. 32pp.

TOPIC: **water sources and uses**

TEACHING FEATURES: **illustrations; cross-sectioned drawings**

The poetic text of this book has only three to nine words per page, yet it effectively describes the water cycle for young children without mentioning the term. Asch's watercolor paintings amplify the sparse text.

Bensen, Laura Lee. 1994. *This Is Our Earth*. Illus. John Carrozza. Watertown, MA: Charlesbridge. 32pp.

TOPIC: **conservation of natural resources**

TEACHING FEATURES: **poetic text; format**

The consistent format of this book—poetry and prose with illustrations—makes it effective and invites rereadings. Each two-page spread includes a section of expository text of ecological significance.

Berger, Melvin. 1994. *Oil Spill!* Illus. Paul Merocha. New York: HarperCollins. 32pp.

TOPIC: **Prince William Sound oil spill**

TEACHING FEATURES: **how-to; labeled drawings; photographs; letter format**

Berger examines the disaster from the perspective of prevention, with dramatic photographs of the oil spill. By including a sample letter to the reader's Senator, he empowers and solicits reader action.

Bernhard, Emery and Durga. 1994. *Eagles: Lions of the Sky*. New York: Holiday House. 32pp.

TOPIC: **eagles**

TEACHING FEATURES: **flow chart; illustrations; captions; glossary; comparison graphs; enlarged drawings; historical significance; borders**

The drawings in this book contain information to digest along with the text. Facts about eagle habits and habitat are illustrated by examples of the eagle as a symbol and the eagle's significance to Native Americans. Even the glossary page, bordered with sixteen different eagle feathers, is worthy of careful study.

Brenner, Barbara, and May Garelick. 1992. *The Tremendous Tree Book*. Illus. Fred Brenner. Honesdale, PA: Boyds Mills Press. 40pp.

TOPIC: **trees**

TEACHING FEATURES: **poetic text; speech balloons; collage**

A raccoon and a squirrel appear in each layout and comment on the information in speech balloons: "Look for baby trees under big trees." "Plant a tree. Squirrels do." The main text is presented in poetic form.

Brown, Don. 1993. *Ruth Law Thrills a Nation*. New York: Ticknor and Fields. 32pp.

TOPIC: **Ruth Law, pioneer aviator**

TEACHING FEATURES: **biography; title**

Ruth Law was a determined woman who lived at a time when "a polite lady always wore a skirt." That's why she had to wear one to the airport over her leather flying suit and hide it in the back of the plane before she took off on her way to aviation history! The book celebrates Ruth Law's 1916 attempt to be the first person to fly from New York to Chicago.

Browne, Philippa Alys. 1995. *African Animals ABC*. San Francisco: Sierra Club Books for Children. 32pp.

TOPIC: **introduction to African animals**

TEACHING FEATURES: **alphabetical organization**

The book begins with "Antbear naps" and ends with "Zebra watches the world go by." With minimal text per page, the author/illustrator takes us through the alphabet to comment on popular and lesser known animals. Her acrylic paintings, in rich, bold colors, add to the informative, respectful view of animals in their African habitat.

Browne, Vee. 1995. *Owl: Animal Lore and Legend*. Illus. Diana Magnuson. New York: Scholastic. 32pp.

TOPIC: **North American owl facts and owl legends**

TEACHING FEATURES: **legend form; effective combination of illustrations, photographs, and artifacts; glossary; maps; captions**

Three Native American legends (from the Seneca, Zuni, and Picuris tribes) are simply told. Each is preceded by several pages of facts about owls, which establish a basis for understanding the legend that follows. The Navajo author gives a unique glimpse of a world, presenting the legends in a way well suited to the older primary child.

Casey, Patricia. 1994. *My Cat Jack*. Cambridge, MA: Candlewick. 28pp.

TOPIC: **cat behaviors**

TEACHING FEATURES: **illustrations**

The Chinese-style ink and watercolor illustrations and minimal text present Jack's behavior in familiar situations. Young children associate the story with personal knowledge and are often prompted to write about their own pets.

Cobb, Vicki. 1990. *Natural Wonders Stories Science Photos Tell*. New York: Lothrop, Lee and Shepard. 32pp.

TOPIC: **scientific photography**

TEACHING FEATURES: **technical photography**

While presenting photographic techniques, Cobb explains scientific phenomena. Photographic techniques include motion, time lapse, polarized light, strobe, micrograph, ultraviolet light, and multiple exposure.

Cohen, Caron Lee. 1996. *Where's the Fly?* Illus. Nancy Barnet. New York: Greenwillow. 32pp.

TOPIC: **a location viewed from larger and larger perspectives**

TEACHING FEATURES: **format; visual perspective; use of questions; border visuals**

The author and illustrator have combined their efforts to help young children understand perspective. Border visuals record changes in perspective to help the reader see that there are many ways to view a particular scene. The book begins on a dog's nose and proceeds to outer space, using only three to six words per page!

Cole, Henry. 1995. *Jack's Garden.* New York: Greenwillow. 28pp.
TOPIC: **changes as a garden grows**
TEACHING FEATURES: **format; labeled illustrations; cutaway drawings; borders; supplemental information page; repetition**
 The format of this book has been effectively planned. The simple repetitive text will draw the youngest readers. Through cutaway drawings, we view the garden and its changes throughout the growing season. The borders extend the text and the main illustration by providing further information through labels.

Cooper, Floyd. 1994. *Coming Home: From the Life of Langston Hughes.* New York: Philomel. 32pp.
TOPIC: **the poet Langston Hughes**
TEACHING FEATURES: **biography**
 Cooper evokes the lonely childhood of Langston Hughes, focusing on the multiple caregivers and homes that nurtured his early years. Although this biography is full of Hughes's disappointments, it is not a story of failure. Cooper shows us how Hughes came to love, appreciate, and understand his people.

Crews, Nina. 1995. *One Hot Summer Day.* New York: Greenwillow. 26pp.
TOPIC: **an urban child's summer day**
TEACHING FEATURES: **photographic collage**
 A photographic collage and minimal text make this hot and humid summer's day real. The resourceful child is immersed in the activities of the inner city. The author conveys an understanding of the limitations and possibilities of the urban setting and meterological basics.

Darling, Kathy. 1996. *Amazon ABC.* Photographs by Tara Darling. New York: Lothrop, Lee and Shepard. 32pp.
TOPIC: **exotic animals of the Amazon Rainforest**
TEACHING FEATURES: **alphabetical organization; pronunciation guide; photography; supplemental information pages; map; labeled drawing**
 A full-page color photograph, the alphabet letter, and the animal name appear on each page. When necessary, the pronunciation follows the name, for example: "zorillo (zor-EE-oh)." The final two pages give brief descriptions of each animal in glossary style. Many of the animals encourage comparison to familiar, related species and identification of similarities and differences.

Day, John. 1995. *Magic.* Photographs by Ziel Mukhida. New York: Thompson Learning. 32pp.
TOPIC: **magic tricks**
TEACHING FEATURES: **how-to; table of contents; index; photographs**
 Children love magic, and this book contains step-by-step directions for fourteen magic tricks. Photographs of child magicians effectively encourage young readers to give it a try.

de Paola, Tomie. 1996. *The Baby Sister.* New York: Putnam. 32pp.
TOPIC: **the birth of a sister**
TEACHING FEATURES: **autobiography**
 De Paola recounts the events in his life at the time of his sister's birth, and

describes his special relationship with his "Nana," who guides him through the experience. A companion to *The Art Lesson* (1989).

Dodson, Peter. 1995. *An Alphabet of Dinosaurs*. Illus. Wayne D. Barlowe. New York: Scholastic. 64pp.

TOPIC: **dinosaurs**

TEACHING FEATURES: **alphabetical organization; supplemental information pages; illustrations; pronunciation guide; typography**

Each double-page spread contains a full-page illustration of the dinosaur in its environment on one side, and two or three facts about the dinosaur in large type as well as a sketch of the skeleton and additional information in smaller type on the other. At the end of the book, a "Guide to Dinosaurs" includes a pronunciation guide and tells what the dinosaur ate, where its fossils were found, and its length.

Drew David. 1992a. *The Book of Animal Records*. Crystal Lake, IL: Rigby. 16pp.

TOPIC: **largest, tallest, fastest animals**

TEACHING FEATURES: **scale diagrams; flow maps; animal location map; photographs; table of contents; index; glossary; abbreviations identification; available as a Big Book**

David Drew packs an amazing amount of information into sixteen pages through visual presentations. He gives readers a reason to return. Children refer to the book when facts from other sources beg comparison. I have observed them comparing information from *Amazing Animals* (1994), which also includes "animal records" but without significant visuals.

Dwight, Laura. 1992. *We Can Do It*. New York: Checkerboard. 32pp.

TOPIC: **everyday activities of five physically and mentally challenged young children**

TEACHING FEATURES: **photographs; repetition; first-person text**

The three- to five-year-olds in this book have various disabilities (including spina bifida, Down syndrome, cerebral palsy, blindness). They are introduced through photograph and text as children who do ordinary work and play with family and friends. Each section begins with "I am ——— and I am ——— years old. I have ——— and I can do lots of things."

Evans, Lisa Gollin. 1992. *An Elephant Never Forgets Its Snorkel: How Animals Survive Without Tools and Gadgets*. Illus. Diane De Groat. New York: Crown. 38pp.

TOPIC: **animal adaptations**

TEACHING FEATURES: **comparative format; title; illustrations; humor**

Contrasting "The Human Way" to accomplish a task (such as carrying groceries home in bags) with "The Animal Way" (stuffing food into cheek pouches), the author supports larger generalizations about adaptation in a clever, entertaining way.

Eversole, Robin. 1995. *Flood Fish*. Illus. Sheldon Greenberg. New York: Crown. 32pp.

TOPIC: **mystery of the Australian flood fish**

TEACHING FEATURES: **use of story; cutaway drawings; author's note**

The story explores the phenomenon of an unusual fish that "appears" inland when the dry riverbeds of Australia flood. "When the puddles dry up, the fish are gone. They leave no bones." A child searches for a scientific explanation and gains insight from family members. The reader is drawn into the investigation along with the story character. An Author's Note supplies current thinking on this issue.

Feldman, Eve B. 1992. *Animals Don't Wear Pajamas*. Illus. Mary Beth Owens. New York: Holt. 32pp.

Topic: **bedtime for animals**

Teaching Features: **title; supplemental information pages; watercolor illustrations**

This book presents the common experience of sleep for sixteen animals. The last two pages add interesting tidbits about the same animals' waking hours.

Filisky, Michael. 1991. *Living Lights: Creatures That Glow in the Dark*. Illus. Katherine Brown-Wing. New York: Crown. 24pp.

Topic: **animals and plants that glow**

Teaching Features: **title; illustrations**

This author builds on children's fascination with animals and plants that glow in the dark. Information about nine, including fireflies, a type of deep sea squid, and a type of mushroom are presented.

First Questions and Answers About Water: Do Fish Drink? 1993. Alexandria, VA: Time-Life for Children. 48pp.

Topic: **water sources, cycle, uses**

Teaching Features: **leading with a question; table of contents; captions; humor; cutaway drawings; speech balloons**

The simplicity of the questions heading each page—"Why does the ocean taste salty, but rivers don't?"—and the illustrations capture the reader. But this book is packed with more information for primary children.

Fraser, Mary Ann. 1996. *Forest Fire*. Golden, CO: Fulcrum. 32pp.

Topic: **the forest fire as a natural event**

Teaching Features: **use of story; illustrations**

Although the author/illustrator portrays the destruction of a naturally caused forest fire, she also sends the message that this disaster is part of nature's cycle. The reader learns of the lodgepole pine, whose resin-coated seeds require intense heat to germinate; the elk, which is nourished by licking ashes; and the hibernating bear, which wakes to feed off animals killed in the fire. This book makes an interesting contrast to Seymour Simon's *Wildfires* (1996).

Gackenback, Dick. 1992. *Mighty Tree*. San Diego, CA: Gulliver. 32pp.

Topic: **the life of three conifers and their function**

Teaching Features: **illustrations**

Through a careful examination of three individual trees, the reader learns how conifers serve nature and man. The book sends an underlying message of conservation while laying a foundation for understanding the significance of the balance of nature.

George, Jean Craighead. 1995. *Everglades.* Illus. Wendell Minor. New York: HarperCollins. 32pp.

TOPIC: **ecological history of the Florida Everglades**

TEACHING FEATURES: **use of story; supplemental information**

George informs and empowers her readers with this story of change. As a storyteller poles his way along through the everglades, he tells his child passengers of the zoological, botanical, and human history of this unique environment and how these histories have affected each other. The children question him about current conditions: "Where are the clouds of egrets?" The storyteller answers with the truth of their sorry fate, but the ending is one of empowerment.

Well-placed wordless illustrations remind us of our collective actions and this vanishing environment.

George, Lindsay Barrett. 1995. *In the Woods: Who's Been Here?* New York: Greenwillow. 44pp.

TOPIC: **finding clues in a woodland to detect the presence of wildlife**

TEACHING FEATURES: **use of story; question format; supplemental information pages; maps**

Lindsay Barrett George goes on a walk with two children and a Golden Retriever to look for signs of wildlife (gnawed branches, a blue feather, tracks in snow). The question "Who lives here?" is effectively asked again and again. The gouache artwork is lifelike and complements the gentle, descriptive text. She is the illustrator of the Long Pond series written by her husband, William T. George.

Gile, John. 1995. *Oh, How I Wished I Could Read!* Illus. Frank Fiorello. Rockford, IL: John Gile. 38pp.

TOPIC: **importance of reading**

TEACHING FEATURES: **poetic text; use of story; fiction in nonfiction; use of humor**

Older primary children will delight in the author's humorous presentation of the plight of a nonreader who finds himself in the dream of a reader. Beyond the humor is a powerful literacy message understandable to those able to read the words "WET PAINT."

Glasser, Linda. 1992. *Wonderful Worms.* Illus. Loretta Krupinski. Brookfield, CT: Milbrook. 32pp.

TOPIC: **the common earthworm**

TEACHING FEATURES: **cutaway drawings; supplemental information pages**

One or two sentences per page teach us about the earthworm's life cycle and behavior. Each page features a below-ground cutaway illustration of the earthworm's environment. A child's feet standing above the focus of the text and illustration provides perspective.

———. 1996. *Compost! Growing Gardens from Your Garbage.* Illus. Anca Hariton. Brookfield, CT: Milbrook. 32pp.

TOPIC: **a family composts**

TEACHING FEATURES: **use of story; supplemental information; first-person narrative**

A young child's family attempts composting. Seen through the eyes of the child, the ecological practice seems easily incorporated into a family's routine. Supplemental information includes important questions and answers about composting.

Godkin, Celia. 1995. *What About Lady Bugs?* San Francisco: Sierra Club. 40pp.

TOPIC: **garden pests**

TEACHING FEATURES: **use of story; enlarged illustrations**

The author/illustrator tells the story of a gardener and his garden. When insects invade, the gardener uses a pesticide. The undesirable result causes the gardener to seek natural pest control in the ladybug. A simple story teaches lessons about ecology, balance of nature, and biological pest control.

Grimes, Niki. 1995. *C Is for City.* Illus. Pat Cummings. New York: Lothrop, Lee and Shepard. 40pp.

TOPIC: **city life**

TEACHING FEATURES: **alphabetical organization; poetic text**

Learn about city life! This is a sophisticated alphabet book for urban children. Those not from the city will learn new terms (for example, "ghetto-blaster sounds," "El train," "double-Dutch," "Kosher shops selling knishes"). The bold acrylic art complements the text.

Guiberson, Brenda. 1991. *Cactus Hotel.* Illus. Megan Lloyd. New York: Holt. 32pp.

TOPIC: **the life cycle of the saguaro cactus and its function as a natural habitat**

TEACHING FEATURES: **title; cross-sectioned drawings; supplemental information pages**

In this book there is a perfect balance, a gentleness, between the text and illustrations. The saguaro's life cycle illustrates the interdependence of nature in the unique desert environment of the American Southwest.

Hall, Zoe. 1994. *It's Pumpkin Time.* Illus. Shari Halpern. New York: Scholastic. 40pp.

TOPIC: **planting and harvesting pumpkins**

TEACHING FEATURES: **use of story; supplemental information pages; illustrations; cross-sectioned drawings; highlighted text**

Shari Halpern's painted paper collage illustrations clearly and simply draw attention to the text, in which two children plant, care for, watch, and wait for their pumpkins to grow. Their goal is to carve jack-o'-lanterns. The final page shows a six-step, cross-sectioned illustration with highlighted text, on "How our pumpkin seeds grow underground."

Hausherr, Rosmarie. 1994. *What Instrument Is This?* New York: Scholastic. 38pp.

TOPIC: **musical instruments**

TEACHING FEATURES: **leading with a question; photographs by the author; design; glossary; labeled drawings; supplemental information pages; typography**

This book effectively alternates color and black-and-white photographs on opposing pages. Each two-page spread begins with a question and a color photograph of a child with an instrument. Each black-and-white "answer" photograph shows the instrument in a "performing environment," and includes the instrument name in bold print and a symbol indicating the group it belongs to (woodwind, brass, etc.). Key words, in italics, can be found in the glossary. The children in the photographs, some with physical disabilities, represent a variety of cultures.

Jim Henson Publishing and the United Nations. 1995. *My Wish for Tomorrow: Words and Pictures from Children Around the World.* New York: Tambourine. 46pp.

TOPIC: **the world's children imagine the future**

TEACHING FEATURES: **foreword; introduction**

This book, with a foreword by Nelson Mandela and an introduction by Boutros Boutros-Ghali, celebrates the fiftieth anniversary of the United Nations. Children from countries around the world express their hopes in their own words.

Highwater, Jamake. 1994. *Songs for the Seasons.* Illus. Sandra Speidel. New York: Lothrop, Lee and Shepard. 32pp.

TOPIC: **seasons**

TEACHING FEATURES: **poetic text**

A red-tailed hawk carries the reader through seasonal scenes of nature illustrated in vivid detail. "Nature's Song. Hear Nature's everlasting song!" The poetic interpretation has appeal for older primary children and for older readers by highlighting observation, appreciation, and delight.

Hines, Anna Grossnickle. 1996. *When We Married Gary.* New York: Greenwillow. 24pp.

TOPIC: **a new stepfather**

TEACHING FEATURES: **biography**

The author tells her young daughter's story of life in a family with a sister and a single mom who subsequently remarries. The five-year-old's perspective, with predicatable fears and observations, will be therapeutic for many children. "Family-album" pages open and conclude the narrative.

Johnson, Jinny. 1995. *Bugs: A Closer Look at the World's Tiny Creatures.* New York: Reader's Digest Kids. 48pp.

TOPIC: **survey of several insect groups**

TEACHING FEATURES: **enlarged photographs; labeled drawings; captions; glossary; index; table of contents; book size**

In this large eleven-by-fourteen-inch book, the full-page photographs of the insects being described have a dramatic impact. Anatomical details emerge clearly. Captioned illustrations of the other members of this insect family surround the illustration.

Kalman, Esther. 1994. *Tchaikovsky Discovers America.* Illus. Laura Fernandez and Rick Jacobson. New York: Orchard Books. 38pp.

TOPIC: **the composer Peter Ilyich Tchaikovsky**

TEACHING FEATURES: **biography; diary format; fiction within a nonfiction work**

A fictional eleven-year-old girl writes about her encounters with Tchaikovsky in her diary, which is based on Tchaikovsky's own diary. More significant than the factual information is the book's portrait of Tchaikovsky as a sensitive dreamer. It also gives attention to his Russian patriotism and contact with expatriate Russians in America.

This book is accessible to primary-age children despite its length, and can be used to accompany exposure to his music. (One illustration depicts him sketching characters as he composes his famous *Nutcracker Suite*.)

Kaplan, John. 1996. *Mom and Me*. New York: Scholastic. 32pp.

TOPIC: **three children and their individual relationships with their mothers**

TEACHING FEATURES: **use of photography; organization by comparison**

Readers are introduced to three children, one by one, as they engage in everyday activities with their mothers. With an emphasis on relationship and emotion, Kaplan effectively spotlights the child-mother relationship in each family.

Kasperson, James. 1995. *Little Brother Moose*. Illus. Karlyn Holman. Nevada City, CA: Dawn. 32pp.

TOPIC: **the impact of human encroachment on moose and their habitat**

TEACHING FEATURES: **use of story; historical introduction; supplemental information pages**

Watercolor illustrations complement this electrifying story, which suggests Native American themes throughout. The reader is engaged in the story from the perspective of a moose, which has painful encounters when lost in the human world of highways and suburban communities. "His stomach told him it was time to eat but he could find no willow tips. There were no laughing streams to follow. Only hard rivers." The reader rejoices when geese point the way home.

King-Smith, Dick. 1995. *All Pigs Are Beautiful*. Illus. Anita Jeram. Cambridge, MA: Candlewick. 32pp.

TOPIC: **characteristics of the pig**

TEACHING FEATURES: **use of story; captions; supplemental information pages**

Pigs are happy, interesting animals, and we should know more about them. The endsheets contain sketches of a dozen types of pigs facing first left and then right. These pen-and-ink and watercolor pictures are whimsical, and the story draws the reader to this member of the animal world.

Kitchen, Bert. 1993. *And So They Build*. Cambridge, MA: Candlewick. 26pp.

TOPIC: **twelve animals who build unusual housing**

TEACHING FEATURES: **typography; illustrations**

The dedication reads "For builders everywhere," and the book celebrates the marvelous ingenuity of birds, termites, mice, insects, spiders, frogs, fish, and beavers as architects and builders. Understanding these creatures through their craft is a refreshing and interesting way to approach them.

Lankford, Mary. 1992. *Hopscotch*. Illus. Karen Milone. New York: Beech Tree. 48pp.

TOPIC: **directions for playing hopscotch from different cultures**

TEACHING FEATURES: **how-to; map; table of contents; index**

The author introduces versions of this childhood game from nineteen cultures. Each includes related facts about the culture and conveys the universal continuity of this simple game. Compared to isolated play in the technological video world, hopscotch suggests a healthy, multicultural option.

Lasky, Kathryn. 1995. *Pond Year*. Illus. Mike Bostock. Cambridge, MA: Candlewick. 28pp.

TOPIC: **seasonal observations and activities at a pond**

TEACHING FEATURES: **use of story; enlarged illustration of focal point**

Two little girls, whose friendship is knitted together by curiosity, love, and respect for nature, play at a neighboring pond. Told in the first person, the girls' observations of pond life are a delight: "Up close, bug parts are amazing and special—just right for each bug." Throughout the seasons, the pond remains a focal point in the children's playful discoveries.

Lauber, Patricia. 1994. *Be a Friend to Trees.* Illus. Holly Keller. New York: HarperCollins. 32pp.

TOPIC: **trees**

TEACHING FEATURES: **labeled drawings; cross-sectioned drawings; supplemental information pages**

The author presents basic scientific facts about trees as a resource for animals and humans. Labeled illustrations support the text, and supplemental information instructs the child with concrete, doable suggestions.

Leigh, Nila K. 1993. *Learning to Swim in Swaziland: A Child's-Eye View of a Southern African Country.* New York: Scholastic. 48pp.

TOPIC: **an eight-year-old American girl relocates in Africa**

TEACHING FEATURES: **autobiography; overall graphic design; labels; maps; combined use of photography and drawings**

"You should not be afraid of what you have never done. You can do all kinds of things you never dreamed you could do. Just like swimming. Just like writing a book. Just like living in Africa." The reader experiences Swaziland through the eyes of an eight-year-old as she shares her fears, triumphs, and adjustments to her new home. The young author makes her adventures real and inviting with drawings and photographs. The book's collage design is a model for young children who find the author's style within their grasp.

Lewin, Betsy. 1995. *Walk a Green Path.* New York: Lothrop, Lee and Shepard. 32pp.

TOPIC: **exotic and common plants**

TEACHING FEATURES: **poetic text; autobiography; format; typography; illustrations; border**

Like pages from the artist's journal, the book presents botanical species, each illustrated by Lewin's watercolors, named and described. Lewin writes about her personal encounters with each species with poetic clarity.

Lewin, Ted. 1996. *Market!* New York: Lothrop, Lee and Shepard. 48pp.

TOPIC: **markets around the world**

TEACHING FEATURES: **comparative organization**

The book takes readers to markets in Ecuador, Nepal, Ireland, Uganda, the United States, and Morocco. At each stop, we are treated to vibrant watercolor illustrations rich with details that demand exploration. Through the common thread of the market, Lewin demonstrates not only the universal need to procure and vend goods, but also the natural resources available in each country. More important, however, is the image of people working in different environments at a common task and the message of world community.

London, Jonathan. 1995. *Honey Paw and Lightfoot.* Illus. Jon Van Zyle. San
Francisco: Chronicle. 36pp.

TOPIC: **life of a mother grizzly bear and her cub**

TEACHING FEATURES: **use of story; supplemental information; poetic text**

London follows the mother grizzly, Honey Paw, from the time she gives
birth to her cub, Lightfoot, until the cub is ready to be independent, conveying
the drama of danger and the warmth of family love. An interesting comparison
is Jon Schoenherr's *Bear* (1991).

Machizui, Ken. 1995. *Baseball Saved Us.* Illus. Dom Lee. New York: Lee and Low. 32pp.

TOPIC: **a Japanese child in an internment camp during World War II**

TEACHING FEATURES: **biography**

Ken Machizui writes a story, based on the internment of his father during
World War II, of the triumph of the human spirit over tragic circumstances. The
game of baseball becomes a link to hope, self-respect, and acceptance.

Markle, Sandra. 1993. *Outside and Inside Trees.* New York: Scholastic. 40pp.

TOPIC: **examination of tree parts**

TEACHING FEATURES: **glossary; index; scientific photography; pronunciation
guide; photographic credits; captions; labels**

This book presents close views of the parts of a tree through scientific photography (enlargement, color enhancement, magnification). The photographic
credits page indicates the degree of magnification (25x), while the combined
glossary-index eases identification. Along with its scientific value, this book is
useful in the classroom for demonstrating the characteristics of the nonfiction
genre.

Marston, Hope Irvin. 1993. *Big Rigs.* New York: Dutton. 48pp.

TOPIC: **trucks**

TEACHING FEATURES: **glossary; cutaway drawings; photographs; leading with a
question; supplemental information page**

Current photographs of modern "rigs" (tractor plus trailer) are featured on
each page with descriptions of various rig combinations. The book concludes
with photographs of the grills and emblems of modern tractor models to teach
the reader how to identify the manufacturer, and a "CB Radio Talk" glossary.

Martin, Jacqueline Briggs. 1995. *Washing the Willow Tree Loon.* Illus. Nancy
Carpenter. New York: Simon and Schuster. 32pp.

TOPIC: **a community attends to birds in danger**

TEACHING FEATURES: **use of story; supplemental information**

After an oil barge leak, a community responds to the plight of affected
loons, which must be rescued and rehabilitated before they can be returned to
the wild. The story drives home the message that we are responsible for pro-
tecting the environment and the wildlife it supports. Readers get a glimpse of
how difficult, perhaps impossible, it is to undo damage to ecosystems.

Micklethwait, Lucy. 1993. *A Child's Book of Art: Great Pictures, First Words.* London:
Dorling Kindersley. 64pp.

TOPIC: **two-dimensional art**

TEACHING FEATURES: **classification organization; instructions for reading; supplemental information pages; typography; labels; table of contents**

The selection of over a hundred paintings from museums and private collections and the organization of this eleven-by-fourteen-inch book make it effective and "user friendly" for children *and* adults. Micklethwait views the world of art through a child's eyes using two-page spreads with simple headings, such as "The Family" or "The Beach." Photographs of paintings on the topic include works of such artists as Coques, van Gogh, Dégas, Renoir, Picasso, Rousseau, Suiseki, and others. Several pages feature a large painting with a series of small oval "cuts" that draw attention to a specific detail.

Miller, Margaret. 1996. *Now I'm Big*. New York: Greenwillow. 22pp.

TOPIC: **children's growth**

TEACHING FEATURES: **photography; highlighted photography**

On every fourth page the same full-page color photograph of the same six children appears. Each time the photograph highlights one of the children by varying the exposure: the entire photograph is underexposed while the "highlighted" child is correctly exposed. Each child presents a different behavior and contrasts behavior as a baby with behavior at six: "When I was a baby I got milk from a bottle and slept in a crib. Now…"

Miller, William. 1994. *Zora Neale Hurston and the Chinaberry Tree*. Illus. Cornelius Van Wright and Ying-Hwa Hu. New York: Lee and Low. 32pp.

TOPIC: **life of the African American writer, Zora Neale Hurston**

TEACHING FEATURES: **biography**

Zora Neale Hurston's childhood relationship with her mother was close and loving. William Miller conveys the devastation and despair Hurston experienced at her mother's untimely death and shows us her determination to use her mother's teaching to "reach for the newborn sky" in her honor. Hurston is a positive role model for children troubled by loss or adversity.

Moutoussamy-Ashe, Jeanne. 1993. *Daddy and Me*. New York: Knopf. 32pp.

TOPIC: **Camera Ashe and her father, Arthur Ashe**

TEACHING FEATURES: **biography; photographs; first-person text**

Written by Camera's mother, the text relates some of the things Camera remembers about her kind and loving father, who was sometimes sick. It highlights their relationship and personal struggle with AIDS, with little mention of Ashe's tennis fame.

Muzik, Katy. 1992. *At Home in the Coral Reef*. Illus. Katherine Brown-Wing. Watertown, MA: Charlesbridge. 32pp.

TOPIC: **creatures at the coral reef**

TEACHING FEATURES: **organization; labeled illustrations; typography**

Creatures depicted in a large photograph on each two-page spread are represented and labeled to the left for closer inspection.

Nail, Jim. 1994. *Whose Tracks Are These? A Clue Book of Familiar Forest Animals*. Illus. Hyla Skudder. Niwot, CT: Roberts Rinehart. 32pp.

TOPIC: **characteristics of forest animals**

TEACHING FEATURES: **use of story; leading with a question**

The author and illustrator take us on a woodland walk, giving clues so the reader can identify the animal before turning the page. This book encourages active participation—a great read-aloud and read-together!

Nichol, Barbara. 1993. *Beethoven Lives Upstairs.* Illus. Scott Cameron. New York: Orchard Books. 48pp.

TOPIC: **the composer Ludwig van Beethoven**

TEACHING FEATURES: **biography; letter writing; use of fiction in a biography**

A fictional young boy writes letters to his uncle about an unusual boarder. Later, it is revealed that the boarder is deaf—and a musical genius! Cameron's oil paintings treat this subject with dignity and respect.

Onyefulu, Ifeoma. 1993. *A Is for Africa.* New York: Cobblehill. 32pp.

TOPIC: **life in an African village (Igbo Tribe, southwestern Nigeria)**

TEACHING FEATURES: **alphabetical organization; photographs**

The reader visits an African village to meet its people and learn about its culture and environment and is taken on a village tour, much as a friend would share her hometown: "*Z* is the rough zigzag lane leading to my village."

Parker, Steve. 1993. *Inside Dinosaurs and Other Prehistoric Creatures.* Illus. Ted Dewan. London: Dorling Kindersley. 48pp.

TOPIC: **anatomy of prehistoric creatures**

TEACHING FEATURES: **cutaway drawings; visual information; humor**

Ted Dewan's illustrations enliven the accompanying facts.

———. 1995. *Dinosaurs! A Spot-the-Difference Puzzle Book.* Illus. Charles Fuge. New York: Random House. 48pp.

TOPIC: **dinosaur scenes**

TEACHING FEATURES: **illustrations; illustrations showing change over time; key**

Two action-packed scenes on facing pages appear identical, but closer inspection proves otherwise. A key provides information on the pages following each set of scenes to describe changes over time. The strength of this book for primary children lies in its unusual use of illustration and the idea that a key can help the reader understand information. The text is probably too difficult for many primary children, but the book lends itself to hours of browsing.

Paulson, Gary. 1995. *The Tortilla Factory.* Illus. Ruth Paulson. New York: Harcourt Brace. 32pp.

TOPIC: **the tortilla in the life cycle of the corn plant**

TEACHING FEATURES: **use of story; poetic text; illustrations**

Oil-on-linen paintings complement rich language. The Paulsons masterfully engage the reader in this story of our reliance on the plant that "give[s] strength to the brown hands that work the black earth." Newberry-acclaimed writer Gary Paulson demonstrates his talent in yet another venue, the picture book.

Pennington, Daniel. 1994. *Itse Selu: Cherokee Harvest Festival.* Illus. Don Stewart. Watertown, MA: Charlesbridge. 34pp.

TOPIC: **Native American celebration**

TEACHING FEATURES: **use of story; pronunciation guide; highlighted words;**

preface; supplemental information pages

This book strives to represent a special day in a Native American village, the Cherokee Harvest Festival. Stewart's powerful illustrations carry the reader to the village and into Little Wolf's family for the event. Viewing the celebration through the experience of a child goes to the heart of its reality and connects the reader with the experience of another culture.

Peters, Lisa Westberg. 1991. *Water's Way*. Illus. Ted Rand. New York: Arcade. 32pp.

TOPIC: **forms of water**

TEACHING FEATURES: **use of story**

In the style of their previous book, *The Sun, the Wind, and the Rain* (Holt 1988), this one weaves together steam, fog, clouds, rain, puddles, ground water, creeks, oceans, frost, and snow: "Water has a way of changing." The message is conveyed through a parallel scientific display. A young boy observes water's varied states at home as nature serves up the identical phenomenon outdoors.

Peterson, Cris. 1994. *Extra Cheese, Please! Mozzarella's Journey from Cow to Pizza*. Photographs by Alvis Upitis. Honesdale, PA: Boyds Mills Press. 32pp.

TOPIC: **milk processed to cheese**

TEACHING FEATURES: **title; first-person text; how-to; recipe; glossary; further reading recommendations; photographs**

The first-person narrative personalizes the story of a cow giving birth and producing milk, and the cheese processing that follows. The reader is offered a personal tour of the farm and a visit with the farm family. Packed with facts ("In one year, she produces 40,000 glasses of milk, enough to make cheese for 1,800 pizzas"), this positive look at farming may make readers change jobs and move!

Peterson-Flemming, Judy, and Bill Flemming. 1996a. *Kitten Training and Critters Too!* Photographs by Darryl Bush. New York: Tambourine. 40pp.

———. 1996b. *Puppy Training and Critters Too!* Photographs by Darryl Bush. New York: Tambourine. 40pp.

TOPIC: **training domestic, marine, and exotic animals**

TEACHING FEATURES: **how-to; photography; typography**

These companion books compare a pet owner teaching a skill (fetch, sit, etc.) to a domestic pet and a professional trainer teaching the same skill to an exotic animal. The young reader can ponder the similarities and differences in the animals that allow comparable training techniques. Each opposing page contains a related fact: "The dark line under a cheetah's eye helps to absorb the glare of the hot sun." The inviting parallels are strengthened by typography and background color.

Pomeroy, Diana. 1996. *One Potato: A Counting Book of Potato Prints*. New York: Harcourt Brace. 28pp.

TOPIC: **how to make potato prints/counting book**

TEACHING FEATURES: **how-to; numerical organization**

Using exquisite, gallery quality potato prints of vegetables, fruits, and flowers, this counting book counts from 1 to 10 followed by 20, 30, 40, 50, and 100.

Instructions for making potato prints extend this book's appeal to include a wider range of readers and would-be artists.

Pratt, Kristen Joy. 1994. *A Swim Through the Sea*. Nevada City, CA: Dawn. 44pp.

TOPIC: **ocean plants and animals**

TEACHING FEATURES: **alphabetical organization; borders; labels**

This alphabet book, by a seventeen-year-old writer, is dedicated "to the children of the Blue Planet—may we work together to protect and preserve its beauty and diversity." She effectively encourages that end by sharing information about ocean life.

Each alphabet letter page features a plant or animal starting with that letter. The borders contain other creatures beginning with the same letter. The text begins with a sentence containing alliteration, followed by further information.

Pringle, Laurence. 1995. *Dinosaurs! Strange and Wonderful*. Illus. Carol Heyer. Honesdale, PA: Boyds Mills Press. 32pp.

TOPIC: **dinosaurs**

TEACHING FEATURES: **typography; pronunciation guide for captions; pronunciation guide within main text**

Bold acrylic illustrations are "action packed," describing the life of the extinct creature in its natural habitat. Modern paleontologists are shown at work. The text uses comparisons young children can understand: "The nests were about as big as your bed."

Reiser, Lynn. 1996. *Beach Feet*. New York: Greenwillow. 32pp.

TOPIC: **beach observation**

TEACHING FEATURES: **organization by categories; captions; typography**

Reiser takes us to the beach to observe feet—human feet and feet of other members of the animal kingdom. Each page features a different kind of feet ("wet cold blue feet," "upside-down feet," printed upside-down). Captions at the bottom of the page are labeled "Footnote" and feature a reduced section from the larger illustration: "A barnacle (Balanus) lies on its back in its shell and kicks its fringed feet up into the water to net food floating by." This book is a must for children who live near a beach—and for those who do not!

Ripley, Catherine. 1995. *Why Is Soap So Slippery? and Other Bathtime Questions*. Illus. Scot Ritchie. Toronto: Owl. 32pp.

TOPIC: **"bathtime questions"**

TEACHING FEATURES: **leading with a question; table of contents without page numbers; labeled drawings; cutaway drawing; humor**

This book takes the reader right into the bathroom with a primary-age child who asks never-ending questions. The answers are accurate, scientific, and to the point. Scot Ritchie's cartoonlike illustrations blend humor and information.

Rockwell, Anne. 1992. *What We Like*. New York: Macmillan. 24pp.

TOPIC: **classification of things children like to do**

TEACHING FEATURES: **classification format; illustrated index; labels**

This is an ideal book for young children and emergent readers. It includes ten kinds of activities (such as "What we like to eat," "What we like to hear,"

"What we like to make"). Labeled illustrations reveal familiar items that fit within the classification.

Rosen, Michael J. 1994. *All Eyes on the Pond*. Illus. Tom Leonard. New York: Hyperion. 32pp.

TOPIC: **pond observation**

TEACHING FEATURES: **enlarged illustrations; insert within illustration; poetic text; perspective**

> In an upper corner of each two-page spread an insert of the enlarged eyes of a pond inhabitant (bird, fish, spider, human, reptile, etc.) shows how it might view the pond. The issue of perspective has value for a wide variety of ages. *Eyes* by Judith Worthy (1988) provides an interesting contrast for younger children.

Ross, Kathy. 1995. *Everyday Is Earth Day*. Illus. Sharon Lane Holm. Brookfield, CT: Milbrook. 48pp.

TOPIC: **art projects using recycled material**

TEACHING FEATURES: **how-to; table of contents; materials list; visual information**

> Not only does this book contain twenty craft projects using recycled materials, it also sprinkles conservation messages throughout. "Damage to our earth is making it hard for many kinds of animals to survive" precedes directions for making a galápagos tortoise out of an old glove and an egg carton. The numbered directions include illustrations to aid young craftspeople.

Ryder, Joanne. 1996. *Jaguar in the Rainforest*. Illus. Michael Rothman. New York: Morrow. 32pp.

TOPIC: **Central American jaguar**

TEACHING FEATURES: **poetic text; use of fiction in nonfiction**

> Through poetry, Joanne Ryder transforms readers into jaguars. Packed with information about the jaguar and its environment, the book is one of many Ryder has produced in this format.

Sadler, Judy Ann. 1995. *Beads*. Toronto: Kids Can Press. 32pp.

TOPIC: **how to make things with beads**

TEACHING FEATURES: **how-to; numbered directions; list of materials; table of contents**

> Directions for making the beads and using them in clever bead projects are presented with clear, step-by-step directions.

Sandved, Kjell B. 1996. *The Butterfly Alphabet*. New York: Scholastic. 64pp.

TOPIC: **pattern in butterfly wings**

TEACHING FEATURES: **micrograph photography; alphabetical organization; visual information; poetic text; supplemental information pages**

> For over twenty-five years and in over thirty countries, the author, a photographer, captured designs on the wings of butterflies and moths, using optical techniques he developed, that suggest the letters of the alphabet. Each letter is a full page photograph. On the facing page, there is a smaller photograph of the entire butterfly or moth and a poetic line in rhyme: for I, "So innocent and unaware, of the riches that they wear." A book for all ages that will motivate children to observe details in nature.

Sayre, April Pulley. 1995. *If You Should Hear a Honey Guide.* Illus. S. D. Schindler.
Boston: Houghton Mifflin. 32pp.

TOPIC: **a Kenyan bird**

TEACHING FEATURES: **use of story; supplemental information; written in the
second person**

The reader travels on a tour of Kenya's wilderness areas guided by the
honey bird. Directed to follow and observe, the reader passes the cobra, elephant, rhino, zebra, and crocodile on the way to the honey guide's favorite
food.

Schertle, Alice. 1995. *Advice for a Frog.* Illus. Norman Green. New York: Lothrop,
Lee and Shepard. 32pp.

TOPIC: **animals**

TEACHING FEATURES: **poetic text; supplemental information pages**

Poet and artist present portraits of fourteen animals. Some poems convey
interesting information ("he stays until the / smooth white bones / are clean"
[vulture]), while others carry an ecological message ("They leave their foot-
prints on this ancient land. / I leave the future buried in the sand." [Galápagos
tortoise]). The last poem addresses the issue of endangered species: "Take a letter, bird: to whom it may concern." The accompanying paintings beg inspection
and further study.

Schimmel, Schim. 1994. *Dear Children of the Earth: A Letter from Home.* Minocqua,
WI: Northword. 32pp.

TOPIC: **conservation**

TEACHING FEATURES: **letter format; use of fiction**

This book's powerful message is delivered by Mother Earth herself: "My
children, tell your friends and other people what I have told you." Captioned
acrylic paintings are bold in color and in their message of responsibility and
empowerment.

Scieszka, Jon. 1995. *Math Curse.* Illus. Lane Smith. New York: Viking. 32pp.

TOPIC: **math in the everyday life of a child**

TEACHING FEATURES: **use of story; humor; typography; visual information**

This wonderfuly outrageous book uses parody and humor to highlight real
math challenges. Readers accompany a girl who sees math challenges everywhere and gets herself tied up in knots with worrying. The author spreads
mathematics thick and thin, so that successive readings reveal new challenges
and new jokes. The dedication is a math problem and the jacket flap uses a Venn
Diagram to indicate other books by the author and illustrator.

Shannon, George. 1996. *Tomorrow's Alphabet.* Illus. Donald Crews. New York:
Greenwillow. 58pp.

TOPIC: **prediction and alphabetic association**

TEACHING FEATURES: **typography; organization**

When I read this book to children, I use a sheet of paper to cover the next
page each time I turn to encourage prediction. "A is for seed—tomorrow's
apple." On facing pages, the letter and the word (*A* and *apple*) appear in large

and brightly colored type. This book is an easy-to-understand example of effective typography for primary and intermediate children.

Silver, Donald. 1994. *One Small Square of Arctic Tundra*. Illus. Patricia Wynne. New York: Freeman. 32pp.

TOPIC: **Arctic tundra**

TEACHING FEATURES: **organization; glossary; index; cross-sectioned drawing; maps; further readings**

This entire book is devoted to the analysis of a six-foot cube of Arctic tundra over a year. Part of each two-page spread discusses experiments (measuring the temperature on and in snow). Other pages illustrate classification (mammals, fish, invertebrates, fungi, plants). This book draws attention to one aspect of scientific inquiry: careful study of a small part of an immense whole.

Sohi, Morteza. 1993. *Look What I Did with a Leaf!* New York: Walker. 32pp.

TOPIC: **how to create pictures from leaves**

TEACHING FEATURES: **how-to; photographs; supplemental information pages**

Sohi shows how to make magnificent animal pictures from pressed leaves. Also included in the book are artist's hints, labeled pictures of leaves sorted according to shape and size, and a leaf field guide. Emergent as well as more experienced readers will scurry to collect leaves!

Wallner, Alexandra. 1995. *Beatrix Potter*. New York: Holiday House. 32pp.

TOPIC: **life of a familiar children's author**

TEACHING FEATURES: **biography; supplemental information; direct quotations**

Alexandra Wallner draws on Beatrix Potter's journals to tell the story of a wealthy but lonely woman who loved nature. She relates the origins of Potter's classic story, *Peter Rabbit*, which was taken from her letters to the son of a former governess, and portrays the time of her life in which her famous children's classics were written.

Whiteley, Opal. 1994. *Only Opal*. Edited by Jane Boulton. Illus. Barbara Cooney. New York: Philomel. 32pp.

TOPIC: **autobiography**

TEACHING FEATURES: **autobiography**

Selections from her diary introduce young readers to orphaned Opal Whiteley (aged five to six) at the beginning of the nineteenth century as she struggles to please her cruel adoptive parents. Her love for the natural world keeps her spirit alive. The story allows children to view events from Opal's perspective.

The text is from the more complete adult version: Opal Whiteley, *Opal: The Journal of an Understanding Heart* (Palo Alto, CA: Tioga, 1984). Both versions preserve Opal's sometimes creative language.

Willow, Diane. 1991. *At Home in the Rain Forest*. Illus. Laura Jacques. Watertown, MA: Charlesbridge. 32pp.

TOPIC: **living things in the rainforest**

TEACHING FEATURES: **endings; labeled illustrations; smaller illustration pulled from a larger one**

The book presents fascinating information about the rain forest's unusual species and the interdependence of all life forms. It concludes with a conservation message.

Wright, Alexandra. 1992. *Will We Miss Them? Endangered Species.* Illus. Marshall Peck III. Watertown, MA: Charlesbridge. 32pp.

TOPIC: **endangered species**

TEACHING FEATURES: **leading with a question; repetition; title; map**

Through its repetition of the introductory question "Will we miss them?", this book elicits an emotional response to the loss of fourteen endangered species. Eleven-year-old Wright repeats her question *before* she presents characteristics of the valued, vanishing animal. This is a powerful book.

Yolen, Jane. 1996. *Welcome to the Sea of Sand.* Illus. Laura Regan. New York: Putnam. 32pp.

TOPIC: **plant and animal life in the desert**

TEACHING FEATURES: **poetic form; pronunciation guide; supplemental information**

Yolen stirs the reader with the beauty of the Sonaran desert in the American southwest. The text and illustrations foster an understanding of this habitat as a unique world teeming with life.

Series Books

Animal Close-Ups Series. Watertown, MA: Charlesbridge.

TOPIC AND TITLE:

The Elephant, Peaceful Giant. 1991. Christine and Michel Denis-Huot.

The Giraffe, A Living Tower. 1992. Christine and Michel Denis-Huot.

The Hippopotamus, River Horse. 1994. Christine and Michel Denis-Huot.

The Cheetah, Fast as Lightning. 1989. Philippe Dupont and Valerie Tracqui.

The Penguin, A Funny Bird. 1992. Beatrice Fontanel.

The Deer, Forest Friend. 1989. Serge and Dominique Simon.

The Seal, Furry Swimmer. 1990. Joelle Soler.

The Bee, Friend of the Flowers. 1991. Paul Starosta.

The Polar Bear, Master of the Ice. 1991. Valerie Tracqui.

TEACHING FEATURES: **series; consistent format; section headings; captions; maps; supplemental information pages; photographs; smaller picture inset in larger one**

The authors provide information to accompany the full-page photographs. One reading gives a simple but clear perspective of the animal's world. The last two pages in each book contain a "Family Album," with photographs and information about the animal's relatives, and "Protection," with discussions of the animal's environmental needs and dangers.

Curious Creatures Series. 1994. Watertown, MA: Charlesbridge. 44pp.

TITLES AND TOPICS:

Animal Bandits. Robert Henno. (magpie, fox, heron, marten, mouse, rat, locust, starling, gull)

Animals in Disguise. Martine Duprez. (camouflage)

Birds of the Night. Jean de Sart. (various owls)

Scary Animals. Jean de Sart. (dangerous animals)

TEACHING FEATURES: **consistent series format; graphic design; title**

Each animal is allotted a two-page prose spread and a page of facts. The information pages are laid out in vertical columns with characteristic headings (natural environment, behavior, voice, reproduction). Many of the two-inch-wide columns include a related illustration. The consistency of the layout is powerful and useful for older primary children in comparing one animal with another.

Eye Openers Series. New York: Aladdin.

TITLES AND TOPICS:

Baby Animals. 1992.

Cars. 1991. Angela Royston.

Diggers and Dump Trucks. 1991.

Dinosaurs. 1991.

Farm Animals. 1991.

Jungle Animals. 1991.

Pets. 1991

Planes. 1992.

Sea Animals. 1992.

Ships and Boats. 1992.

Trucks. 1991.

Zoo Animals. 1991.

TEACHING FEATURES: **photographs; illustrations; enlarged drawings; labeling; borders**

Each book features a cutout of a large photograph of the topic explored, set on a white background for emphasis. The text is simple and the print large. Young readers delight in this presentation.

Johnson, Jinny. 1991. Highlights Animal Books Series. Columbus, OH: Highlights.

TOPICS AND TITLES:

Eagles

Elephants

Pandas

Seals

Tigers

TEACHING FEATURES: **consistent series format; table of contents; headings; photographs and illustrations; captions; supplemental information inserts; enlarged illustrations; use of fiction; index; labels; typography**

These inexpensive softcover books hold a lot of information! They introduce many of the features of nonfiction by presenting facts about interesting animals. They also use fiction, which is unusual in a series format.

Pallotta, Jerry. Alphabet Books Series. Watertown, MA: Charlesbridge. 32pp.

TOPICS AND TITLES:

The Bird Alphabet Book. 1986.

The Butterfly Alphabet Book. 1995.

The Desert Alphabet Book. 1994.

The Dinosaur Alphabet Book. 1991.

The Extinct Alphabet Book. 1993.

The Flower Alphabet Book. 1988.

The Frog Alphabet Book. 1990.

The Furry Alphabet Book. 1991.

The Icky Bug Counting Book. 1992.

The Ocean Alphabet Book. 1986.

The Underwater Alphabet Book. 1991.

The Victory Garden Vegetable Alphabet Book. 1992.

The Yucky Reptile Alphabet Book. 1989.

TEACHING FEATURES: **alphabetical organization; consistent format; typography; illustrations; title**

Children love these books! Useful for reference, they entertain as well. Pallotta includes the familiar and unfamiliar for the alphabet book browser. The final page in each book has extra information or some clever ending: "Sorry, Naked Mole Rat. You are a mammal, but you do not have any fur, and you are also quite ugly. You should not be in this book, not even at THE END" (*The Furry Alphabet Book*, 1991).

Rowe, Julian, and Molly Perham. 1993. First Science Series. Chicago: Children's Press. 32pp.

TOPICS AND TITLES:

Colorful Light

Feel and Touch!

Keep It Afloat!

Keeping Your Balance

Make It Move!

Making Sounds

TOPIC: **ways things move**

TEACHING FEATURES: **index; table of contents; format; photographs; drawings; how-to**

This series of books makes scientific topics understandable to young children. They offer a concept like levers by first showing photographs of children engaged in a lever-related problem or activity using a lever. This is followed by a "how-to" page with simple, illustrated instructions for a related experiment with safe but common materials. All concepts are presented in varied situations that are within the realm of children's experience.

See How They Grow Series. 1991–1992. New York: Lodestar.

TITLES AND TOPICS:

Butterfly. 1992. Mary Ling.

Chick. 1992.

Duck. 1991.
Foal. 1992. Mary Ling.
Fox. 1992. Mary Ling.
Frog. 1991.
Kitten. 1991.
Lamb. 1992.
Mouse. 1992.
Owl. 1992. Mary Ling.
Puppy. 1991.
Rabbit. 1991.
TEACHING FEATURES: **photographs; labeling; borders; summary page**

Cutout photographs on each page are accompanied by a clever first-person text. The page borders depict the growth described in the text. The summary page, which gathers together one picture from each page, ties together age and development.

Glossary

ability mental or physical competence.

auditory relating to the sense of hearing.

autobiography the author's account of his or her life.

author study a full or partial review of an author's work to develop a sense of familiarity with the author's characteristic style, genre, and subject matter.

behavior a controlled or uncontrolled physical or mental action.

biography an account of another person's life or part of that life.

Caldecott Medal an annual award of the Association for Library Services to Children (American Library Association) to the outstanding American picture book for children.

classify the act of systematic sorting by identifiable character.

cognitive reference to a mental function.

competence ability to carry out a task.

conference a professional occasion for presenting new research; also, dialogue on a specific subject to seek guidance.

content area a body of knowledge with specialized vocabulary such as science, mathematics, or social studies.

creative the ability to identify and solve problems and react to new ideas or problems.

cross-sectioned drawing a drawing depicting internal structure from a two-dimensional perspective.

curriculum the planned experiences of a school program.

cutaway drawing a drawing depicting internal structure from a three-dimensional perspective.

dialogue verbal communication between two or more people.

direct documentation observations, comments, conclusions, or questions recorded by a professional as a result of personal interaction; also referred to as anecdotal notes (Johnston 1993a).

disabled requiring additional support in order to participate in a given activity because of factors having a physical, emotional, or intellectual origin.

empathy the ability to understand or identify with another individual's feelings or thoughts.

environment surroundings, things, conditions, and influences that can affect the individual.

fiction imaginative narrative text.

genre a classification of literature having a common format and intent.

goal an objective or target on which to focus effort.

graphic design the final appearance of the work: text position, spacing, size, and type combined with visual information in the final product.

learning a process in which behavior is altered and knowledge gained through instruction or experience.

literacy a level of language competence that allows an individual to function and participate meaningfully within a society.

mini-lesson a brief instruction preceding a reading or writing workshop on a topic of importance to the group.

nonfiction a literary genre whose primary purpose is to inform or convince.

portfolio samples of work collected, focused, and organized by the learner to depict growth, achievement, and direction.

primary-age children children who are five, six, seven, and eight years old.

research focused systematic inquiry.

series book a book written as a part of a collection of similar books in the same genre on related topics.

typography the style or appearance of printed matter, which may enhance or organize the text.

verbal having to do with oral language.

visual relating to the sense of sight.

visual information presentation included within or in place of text in a visual form (graphs, maps, time lines, diagrams, flow charts, and time lines).

References

Children's Books Cited

Adler, David A. 1990. *A Picture Book of Helen Keller*. New York: Holiday House.

Archambault, John. 1996. *The Birth of a Whale*. Parsippany, NJ: Silver Press.

Arnosky, Jim. 1993. *Crinkleroot's 25 Fish Every Child Should Know*. New York: Bradbury Press.

Asch, Frank. 1982. *Happy Birthday, Moon*. New York: Prentice-Hall.

———. 1985. *Bear Shadow*. New York: Scholastic.

———. 1995. *Water*. New York: Harcourt Brace.

Back, Christine, and Barrie Watts. 1984. *Bean and Plant*. Englewood Cliffs, NJ: Silver Burdett.

Barton, Byron. 1981. *Building a House*. New York: Greenwillow.

———. 1990. *Bones, Bones, Dinosaur Bones*. New York: Crowell.

Beaton, Clare. 1990. *Face Painting*. New York: Watts.

Bedik, Shelley. 1993. *Our President: Bill Clinton*. New York: Scholastic.

Bell, Simon, and Alexandra Parsons, eds. 1991. *What's Inside My Body?* London: Dorling Kindersley.

Bensen, Laura Lee. 1994. *This Is Our Earth*. Illus. John Carrozza. Watertown, MA: Charlesbridge.

Berger, Melvin. 1994. *Oil Spill!* New York: HarperCollins.

Bernhard, Emery and Durga. 1994. *Eagles: Lions of the Sky*. New York: Holiday House.

Biesty, Stephen. 1993. *Cross-Sections Man-of-War*. London: Dorling Kindersley.

Brenner, Barbara, and May Garelick. 1992. *The Tremendous Tree Book*. Honesdale, PA: Boyds Mills Press.

Brenner, Richard J. 1994. *Shaquille O'Neal*. Syosset, NY: East End.

Brett, Jan. 1985. *Annie and the Wild Animals*. Boston: Houghton Mifflin.

Brown, Don. 1993. *Ruth Law Thrills a Nation*. New York: Ticknor and Fields.

Browne, Philippa Alys. 1995. *African Animals ABC*. San Francisco: Sierra Club Books for Children.

Browne, Vee. 1995. *Owl: Animal Lore and Legend*. New York: Scholastic.

Burleigh, Robert. 1991. *Flight: The Journey of Charles Lindbergh*. New York: Putnam and Grosset.

Burns, Marilyn. 1994. *The Greedy Triangle*. New York: Scholastic.

Carle, Eric. 1987. *The Tiny Seed*. Natick, MA: Picture Book Studio.

Casey, Patricia. 1994. *My Cat Jack*. Cambridge, MA: Candlewick.

Cobb, Vicki. 1990. *Natural Wonders: Stories Science Photos Tell*. New York: Lothrop, Lee and Shepard.

REFERENCES   Cohen, Caron Lee. 1996. *Where's the Fly?* New York: Greenwillow.

Cole, Henry. 1995. *Jack's Garden.* New York: Greenwillow.

Cole, Joanna. 1990. *The Magic School Bus Lost in the Solar System.* New York: Scholastic.

———. 1995. *My New Kitten.* New York: Morrow.

Cooper, Floyd. 1994. *Coming Home: From the Life of Langston Hughes.* New York: Philomel.

Cousteau Society. 1992. *Manatees.* New York: Simon and Schuster.

Crews, Donald. 1980. *Trucks.* New York: Greenwillow.

Crews, Nina. 1995. *One Hot Summer Day.* New York: Greenwillow.

Darling, Kathy. 1996. *Amazon ABC.* New York: Lothrop, Lee and Shepard.

d'Aulaire, Ingri and Edgar P. 1939. *Abraham Lincoln.* New York: Doubleday.

Day, John. 1995. *Magic.* New York: Thompson.

Demarest, Chris. 1993. *Lindbergh.* New York: Crown.

de Paola, Tomie. 1973. *Nana Upstairs, Nana Downstairs.* New York: Putnam.

———. 1976. *Things to Make and Do on Valentine's Day.* New York: Franklin Watts.

———. 1981. *One Foot Now the Other.* New York: Putnam.

———. 1989a. *The Art Lesson.* New York: Putnam.

———. 1989b. "The Secret Place," *Tomie de Paola's Book of Poems.* London: Methuen.

———. 1996. *The Baby Sister.* New York: Putnam.

Dewitt, Jamie. 1984. *Jamie's Turn.* Milwaukee, WI: Raintree.

Dodson, Peter. 1995. *An Alphabet of Dinosaurs.* New York: Scholastic.

Drew, David. 1992a. *The Book of Animal Records.* Crystal Lake, IL: Rigby.

———. 1992b. *What Did You Eat Today?* Crystal Lake, IL: Rigby.

Dwight, Laura. 1992. *We Can Do It.* New York: Checkerboard.

Ehlert, Lois. 1987. *Growing Vegetable Soup.* Orlando, FL: Harcourt Brace.

Evans, Lisa Gollin. 1992. *An Elephant Never Forgets Its Snorkel: How Animals Survive Without Tools and Gadgets.* New York: Crown.

Eversole, Robin. 1995. *Flood Fish.* New York: Crown.

Feldman, Eve B. 1992. *Animals Don't Wear Pajamas.* New York: Holt.

Filisky, Michael. 1991. *Living Lights: Creatures That Glow in the Dark.* New York: Crown.

First Questions and Answers About Water: Do Fish Drink? 1993. Alexandria, VA: Time-Life for Children.

Ford, Miela. 1995. *Sunflower.* New York: Greenwillow.

Fraser, Mary Ann. 1996. *Forest Fire!* Golden, CO: Fulcrum.

Gackenback, Dick. 1992. *Mighty Tree.* San Diego, CA: Gulliver.

Gaes, Jason. 1987. *My Book for Kids with Cansur.* Aberdeen, SD: Melius and Peterson.

Gates, Frieda. 1978. *Glove, Mitten, and Sock Puppets.* New York: Scholastic.

Gelman, Rita G. 1992. *Body Battles.* New York: Scholastic.

Gemme, L. B. 1978. *T-Ball Is Our Game.* Chicago: Children's Press.

George, Jean Craighead. 1995. *Everglades.* New York: HarperCollins.

George, Lindsay Barrett. 1995a. *In the Snow: Who's Been Here?* New York: Greenwillow.

———. 1995b. *In the Woods: Who's Been Here?* New York: Greenwillow.

Gibbons, Gail. 1981. *Trucks*. New York: Crowell.

———. 1987. *The Pottery Place*. New York: Harcourt Brace.

———. 1989. *Monarch Butterfly*. New York: Holiday House.

———. 1990. *How a House Is Built*. New York: Holiday House.

———. 1991a. *From Seed to Plant*. New York: Holiday House.

———. 1991b. *The Puffins Are Back*. New York: Holiday House.

———. 1991c. *Whales*. New York: Holiday House.

———. 1992a. *Say Woof: The Day of a Country Veterinarian*. New York: Holiday House.

———. 1992b. *Sharks*. New York: Holiday House.

Gile, John. 1995. *Oh, How I Wished I Could Read!* Rockford, IL: John Gile.

Glasser, Linda. 1992. *Wonderful Worms*. Brookfield, CT: Milbrook.

———. 1996. *Compost! Growing Gardens from Your Garbage*. Brookfield, CT: Milbrook.

Godkin, Celia. 1995. *What About Lady Bugs?* San Francisco: Sierra Club.

Gofstein, M. B. 1989. *A Little Schubert*. New York: Trumpet.

Goldish, Meish. 1992. *Paper Party*. New York: Macmillan Big Books.

Gomboli, Mario. 1994. *Amazing Animals*. London: Binky.

Grimes, Niki. 1995. *C Is for City*. Illus. Pat Cummings. New York: Lothrop, Lee and Shepard.

Grosshandler, Henry and Janet. 1990. *Everyone Wins at Tee Ball*. New York: Dutton.

Guiberson, Brenda. 1991. *Cactus Hotel*. New York: Holt.

Hall, Zoe. 1994. *It's Pumpkin Time*. New York: Scholastic.

Hausherr, Rosmarie. 1994. *What Instrument Is This?* New York: Scholastic.

Heller, Ruth. 1983. *The Reason for a Flower*. New York: Putnam.

Jim Henson Publishing and the United Nations. 1995. *My Wish for Tomorrow: Words and Pictures from Children Around the World*. New York: Tambourine.

Highwater, Jamake. 1994. *Songs for the Seasons*. New York: Lothrop, Lee and Shepard.

Hines, Anna Grossnickle. 1996. *When We Married Gary*. New York: Greenwillow.

Hirschi, Ron. 1986. *One Day on Pika's Peak*. New York: Dodd, Mead.

———. 1989. *Who Lives in the Mountains?* New York: Putnam.

Hogan, Paul. 1979. *The Dandelion*. Milwaukee, WI: Raintree.

Houston, Gloria. 1992. *My Great-Aunt Arizona*. New York: HarperCollins.

Hutchins, Pat. 1971. *Titch*. New York: Macmillan.

Iverson, Diane. 1993. *I Celebrate Nature*. Nevada City, CA: Dawn.

Johnson, Jinny. 1995. *Bugs: A Closer Look at the World's Tiny Creatures*. New York: Reader's Digest Kids.

Kaizuki, Kiyonori. 1988. *A Calf Is Born*. New York: Orchard Books.

Kalman, Esther. 1994. *Tchaikovsky Discovers America*. New York: Orchard Books.

Kaplan, John. 1996. *Mom and Me*. New York: Scholastic.

Kasperson, James. 1995. *Little Brother Moose*. Illus. Karlyn Holman. Nevada City, CA: Dawn.

Kessler, Cristina. 1995. *All the King's Animals: The Return of Endangered Wildlife to Swaziland*. Honesdale, PA: Boyds Mills Press.

REFERENCES

King-Smith, Dick. 1995. *All Pigs Are Beautiful*. Cambridge, MA: Candlewick.

Kitchen, Bert. 1993. *And So They Build*. Cambridge, MA: Candlewick.

Krauss, Ruth. 1945. *The Carrot Seed*. New York: HarperCollins.

Kumin, Maxine. 1984. *The Microscope*. New York: HarperCollins.

Kuskin, Karla. 1982. *The Philharmonic Gets Dressed*. New York: HarperCollins.

Lankford, Mary. 1992. *Hopscotch*. New York: Beech Tree.

Lasky, Kathryn. 1995. *Pond Year*. Cambridge, MA: Candlewick.

Lauber, Patricia. 1994. *Be a Friend to Trees*. New York: HarperCollins.

Leigh, Nila K. 1993. *Learning to Swim in Swaziland: A Child's-Eye View of a Southern African Country*. New York: Scholastic.

Lewin, Betsy. 1995. *Walk a Green Path*. New York: Lothrop, Lee and Shepard.

Lewin, Ted. 1996. *Market!* New York: Lothrop, Lee and Shepard.

London, Jonathan. 1995. *Honey Paw and Lightfoot*. San Francisco: Chronicle.

Loomis, Christine. 1993. *In the Diner*. New York: Scholastic.

Maccarone, Grace. 1995. *Monster Math*. New York: Scholastic.

Machizui, Ken. 1995. *Baseball Saved Us*. New York: Lee and Low.

MacMillan, Bruce. 1986. *Counting Wildflowers*. New York: Morrow.

———. 1991. *Eating Fractions*. New York: Scholastic.

———. 1992. *Going on a Whale Watch*. New York: Scholastic.

MacMillan, Dianne. 1993. *Chinese New Year*. Hillside, NJ: Enslow.

"Make a Quake." *Scholastic News* 51, (7): 1 and 4.

Markle, Sandra. 1991. *Outside and Inside You*. New York: Scholastic.

———. 1993. *Outside and Inside Trees*. New York: Scholastic.

Marston, Hope Irvin. 1993. *Big Rigs*. New York: Dutton.

Martin, Jacqueline Briggs. 1995. *Washing the Willow Tree Loon*. New York: Simon and Schuster.

Martin, Louise. 1988. *Whales*. Vero Beach, FL: Rourke.

Martin, Patricia. 1969. *Jacqueline Kennedy Onassis*. New York: Putnam.

Marzollo, Jean. 1991. *In 1492*. New York: Scholastic.

———. 1993. *Happy Birthday, Martin Luther King*. New York: Scholastic.

McMahon, Patricia. 1995. *Listen for the Bus: David's Story*. Honesdale, PA: Boyds Mills Press.

Micklethwait, Lucy. 1993. *A Child's Book of Art: Great Pictures, First Words*. London: Dorling Kindersley.

Micucci, Charles. 1992. *The Life and Times of the Apple*. New York: Orchard Books.

Miller, Margaret. 1996. *Now I'm Big*. New York: Greenwillow.

Miller, William. 1994. *Zora Hurston and the Chinaberry Tree*. New York: Lee and Low.

Mitchell, Robert, and Herbert Zim. 1964. *Butterflies and Moths*. Racine, WI: Western.

Morris, Ann. 1989. *Hats Hats Hats*. New York: Scholastic.

Moutoussamy-Ashe, Jeanne. 1993. *Daddy and Me*. New York: Knopf.

Muzik, Katy. 1992. *At Home in the Coral Reef*. Illus. Katherine Brown-Wing. Watertown, MA: Charlesbridge.

Nail, Jim. 1994. *Whose Tracks Are These? A Clue Book of Familiar Forest Animals*. Niwot, CT: Roberts Rinehart.

National Wildlife Federation. *Ranger Rick*. Magazine published by National Wildlife Federation.

———. *Your Big Backyard*. Magazine published by National Wildlife Federation.

———. 1981. "The Pika." *Your Big Backyard*. Magazine published by National Wildlife Federation.

———. 1988. *The Unhuggables*. Vienna, VA: National Wildlife Federation.

Nichol, Barbara. 1993. *Beethoven Lives Upstairs*. New York: Orchard Books.

Onyefulu, Ifeoma. 1993. *A Is for Africa*. New York: Cobblehill.

Parish, Peggy. 1974. *Dinosaur Time*. New York: Scholastic.

Parker, Steve. 1993. *Inside Dinosaurs and Other Prehistoric Creatures*. London: Dorling Kindersley.

———. 1995. *Dinosaurs! A Spot-the-Difference Puzzle Book*. New York: Random House.

Paulson, Gary. 1995. *The Tortilla Factory*. Illus. Ruth Paulson. New York: Harcourt Brace.

Pennington, Daniel. 1994. *Itsu Selu: Cherokee Harvest Festival*. Watertown, MA: Charlesbridge.

Peters, Lisa Westberg. 1991. *Water's Way*. New York: Arcade.

Peterson, Cris. 1994. *Extra Cheese, Please! Mozzarella's Journey from Cow to Pizza*. Honesdale, PA: Boyds Mills Press.

Peterson-Flemming, Judy, and Bill Flemming. 1996a. *Kitten Training and Critters Too!* New York: Tambourine.

———. 1996b. *Puppy Training and Critters Too!* New York: Tambourine.

Pinczes, Elinor. 1993. *One Hundred Hungry Ants*. Boston: Houghton Mifflin.

Pomeroy, Diana. 1996. *One Potato: A Counting Book of Potato Prints*. New York: Harcourt Brace.

Pratt, Kristen Joy. 1994. *A Swim Through the Sea*. Nevada City, CA: Dawn.

Pretlutsky, Jack. 1988. *Tyrannosaurus Was a Beast*. New York: Greenwillow.

Pringle, Laurence. 1995. *Dinosaurs! Strange and Wonderful*. Illus. Carol Heyer. Honesdale, PA: Boyds Mills Press.

Rahaniotis, Angela, and Jane Brierley, eds. 1994. *It's a Big, Big World Atlas*. Montreal: Tormondt.

Reid, George. 1967. *Pond Life*. Racine, WI: Western.

Reiser, Lynn. 1996. *Beach Feet*. New York: Greenwillow.

Rhodes, Frank, et al. 1962. *Fossils: A Guide to Prehistoric Life*. Racine, WI: Western.

Ripley, Catherine. 1995. *Why Is Soap So Slippery? and Other Bathtime Questions*. Toronto: Owl.

Rockwell, Anne. 1989a. *Apples and Pumpkins*. New York: Macmillan.

———. 1989b. *Bear Child's Book of Special Days*. New York: Dutton.

———. 1992a. *Our Yard Is Full of Birds*. New York: Macmillan.

———. 1992b. *What We Like*. New York: Macmillan.

Roop, Peter and Connie. 1985. *Keep the Lights Burning, Abbie*. Minneapolis, MN: Carolrhoda.

Rosen, Michael J. 1994. *All Eyes on the Pond*. New York: Hyperion.

REFERENCES

Ross, Kathy. 1995. *Every Day Is Earth Day*. Brookfield, CT: Millbrook.

Ryder, Joanne. 1996. *Jaguar in the Rainforest*. New York: Morrow.

Sadler, Judy Ann. 1995. *Beads*. Toronto: Kids Can Press.

Sandved, Kjell B. 1996. *The Butterfly Alphabet*. New York: Scholastic.

Sayre, April Pulley. 1995. *If You Should Hear a Honey Guide*. Boston: Houghton Mifflin.

Scarey, Richard. 1963. *Richard Scarey's Best Word Book Ever*. New York: Golden Press.

Schertle, Alice. 1995. *Advice for a Frog*. New York: Lothrop, Lee and Shepard.

Schimmel, Schim. 1994. *Dear Children of the Earth: A Letter from Home*. Minocqua, WI: Northword.

Schlank, Carol H., and Barbara Metzger. 1991. *Elizabeth Cady Stanton: A Biography for Young Children*. Mt. Rainer, MD: Gryphon House.

Scieszka, Jon. 1995. *Math Curse*. Illus. Lane Smith. New York: Viking.

Sharratt, Nick. 1994. *My Mom and Dad Make Me Laugh*. Cambridge, MA: Candlewick.

Silver, Donald. 1994. *One Small Square of Arctic Tundra*. New York: Freeman.

Simon, Seymour. 1988. *Volcanoes*. New York: Mulberry.

———. 1989. *Whales*. New York: Crowell.

———. 1991. *Earthquakes*. New York: Morrow.

———. 1996. *Wildfires*. New York: Morrow.

Sims, Doris. 1980. *Stop and Go: Garret Morgan, Inventor*. Los Angeles: Children's Cultu-Lit.

Slater, Teddy. 1996. *Stay in Line*. Illus. Gioia Fiammenghi. New York: Scholastic.

Snapshot Books. 1994. *Things on Wheels*. New York: Covent Garden.

Sohi, Morteza. 1993. *Look What I Did with a Leaf!* New York: Walker.

Steele, Mary. 1987. *Anna's Garden Songs*. New York: Scholastic.

"This City Needs Help." 1995. *Scholastic News* 51, (7): 1.

Titherington, Jan. 1986. *Pumpkin, Pumpkin*. New York: Greenwillow.

Turner, Barrie. 1989. *I Like Music*. New York: Warwick.

Walker, Colin. 1992. *Seeds Grow*. Bothell, WA: Wright Group.

Wallner, Alexandra. 1995. *Beatrix Potter*. New York: Holiday House.

Waters, Kate. 1990. *Lion Dancer: Ernie Wan's Chinese New Year*. Illus. Madeline Slovenz-Low. New York: Scholastic.

Whiteley, Opal. 1984. *Opal: The Journal of an Understanding Heart*. Palo Alto, CA: Tioga.

———. 1994. *Only Opal*. New York: Philomel.

Willow, Diane. 1991. *At Home in the Rain Forest*. Watertown, MA: Charlesbridge.

Winston, Mary, ed. 1993. *American Heart Association Kids' Cookbook*. New York: Random House.

Wolf, Bernard. 1995. *Homeless*. New York: Orchard Books.

Worthy, Judith. 1988. *Eyes*. Littleton, MA: Sundance.

Wright, Alexandra. 1992. *Will We Miss Them? Endangered Species*. Watertown, MA: Charlesbridge.

Yolen, Jane. 1996. *Welcome to the Sea of Sand*. New York: Putnam.

Zim, Herbert, and Clarence Cotton. 1987. *Insects: A Guide to Familar American Insects*. Racine, WI: Western.

Series Books

Animal Close-Ups Series. 1989–1991. Watertown, MA: Charlesbridge.
Curious Creature Series. 1994. Watertown, MA: Charlesbridge.
Eye Openers Series. 1991–1992. New York: Aladdin.
Greene, Carol. 1993. *Reading About the Manatee*. Friends in Danger Series. Hillside, NJ: Enslow.
Highlights Animal Book Series. 1991. Columbus, OH: Highlights.
Pallotta, Jerry. 1986–1995. Alphabet Series. Watertown, MA: Charlesbridge.
Rowe, Julian and Molly. 1993. First Science Series. Chicago: Children's Press.
Scholastic First Discovery Books. 1990. *Castles*. New York: Scholastic.
———. 1992. *Musical Instruments*. New York: Scholastic.
See How They Grow Series. 1991–1992. New York: Lodestar.

Professional References

Atwell, Nancie. 1987. *In the Middle: Writing, Reading, and Learning with Adolescents*. Portsmouth, NH: Boynton/Cook.
Avery, Carol. 1993. *And with a Light Touch: Learning About Reading, Writing, and Teaching with First Graders*. Portsmouth, NH: Heinemann.
Calkins, Lucy. 1986. *The Art of Teaching Writing*. Portsmouth, NH: Heinemann.
Carson, Rachel. 1956. *The Sense of Wonder*. New York: HarperCollins.
Duthie, Christine, and Ellie Zimet. 1993. "Poetry Is Like Directions for Your Imagination." *Reading Teacher* 45: 14–24.
Fletcher, Ralph. Address to New York State Reading Association Annual Conference, Kiamesha Lake, NY, 5 Nov. 1992.
Fritz, Jean. 1988. "Biography: Readability Plus Responsibility." *The Horn Book* 6: 759–760.
Garland, Cynthia. 1988. *Mathematics Their Way*. Summary Newsletter. Saratoga, CA: Center for Innovation in Education.
Goodman, Yetta, Dorothy Watson, and Carolyn Burke. 1984. *Reading Strategies: Focus on Comprehension*. New York: Richard C. Owen.
Graves, Donald. 1989. *Investigate Nonfiction*. Portsmouth, NH: Heinemann.
Grolier. 1993. *The New Grolier Multimedia Encyclopedia: The Academic American Encyclopedia*. CD-ROM. Danbury, CT: Grolier.
Hansen, Jane. 1987. *When Writers Read*. Portsmouth, NH: Heinemann.
Johnston, Peter. 1992. "Nontechnical Assessment." *Reading Teacher* 46: 60–62.
———. 1993a. "Assessment and Literate 'Development.'" *Reading Teacher* 46: 428–429.

REFERENCES ———. 1993b. "Constructive Evaluation." Address, University of New Hampshire, 19 July 1993.

Lee, Enid. 1994. "Taking Multicultural Education Seriously." In *Rethinking Our Classrooms: Teaching for Equity and Justice*. B. Bigelow, L. Christensen, S. Karp, B. Miner, and B. Peterson eds. pp. 19–22. Milwaukee, WI: Rethinking Schools Limited.

Manning, John C. 1995. "Ariston Metron." *Reading Teacher* 48: 650–660.

Moline, Steve. 1995. *I See What You Mean: Children at Work with Visual Information*. York, ME: Stenhouse.

Moore, Rena. 1989. "Fossil Hunters: Relating Reading, Writing, and Science." In *Workshop 1: By and for Teachers*. Nancie Atwell, ed. pp. 103–109. Portsmouth, NH: Heinemann.

Papert, Seymour. 1993. *The Children's Machine: Rethinking School in the Age of the Computer*. New York: Basic Books.

Rief, Linda. 1985. "Why Can't We Live Like the Monarch Butterfly?" In *Breaking Ground: Teachers Relate Reading and Writing in the Elementary School*. Jane Hansen, Thomas Newkirk, and Donald Graves, eds. Portsmouth, NH: Heinemann.

Saul, Wendy, et al. 1993. *Science Workshop: A Whole Language Approach*. Portsmouth, NH: Heinemann.

Sawyer, W. E., and D. E. Comer. 1991. *Growing Up with Literature*. Albany, NY: Delmar.

Smith, Frank. 1986. *Insult to Intelligence: The Bureaucratic Invasion of Our Classroom*. New York: Arbor House.

Stowell, Charlotte. 1994. *Step-by-Step: Making Books*. New York: Kingfisher.

Strickland, Dorothy. 1995. "Reinventing Our Literacy Programs: Books, Basics, Balance." *Reading Teacher* 48: 294–302.

Vardell, Sylvia, and Kathleen Copeland. 1992. "Reading Aloud and Responding to Nonficiton: Let's Talk About It." In *Using Nonfiction Trade Books in the Elementary Classroom*. E. B. Freeman and D. G. Person, eds. Urbana, IL: National Council of Teachers of English.

Vygotsky, L. S. 1978. *Mind and Society: The Development of Higher Psychological Processes*. Michael Cole, Vera John-Steiner, Sylvia Scribner, and Ellen Souberman, eds. Cambridge, MA: Harvard University Press.

Whitin, David, and Sandra Wilde. 1992. *Read Any Good Math Lately? Children's Books for Mathematical Learning, K–6*. Portsmouth, NH: Heinemann.

Wood, Chip. 1994. *Yardsticks*. Greenfield, MA: Northeast Foundation for Children.

Wright, June, and Daniel Shade, eds. 1994. *Young Children: Active Learners in a Technological Age*. Washington, DC: National Association for the Education of Young Children.

Zarnowski, Myra. 1990. *Learning About Biographies*. Urbana, IL: National Council of Teachers of English.